Ocean City
ODDITIES

KRISTIN HELF & BRANDON SEIDL

THE
History
PRESS

Published by The History Press
Charleston, SC
www.historypress.com

First published 2020

Manufactured in the United States

ISBN 9781467142465

Library of Congress Control Number: 2020930476

Notice: The information in this book is true and complete to the best of our knowledge. It is offered without guarantee on the part of the authors or The History Press. The authors and The History Press disclaim all liability in connection with the use of this book.

In Memory of H. Michael Heath and Christopher Morgan Trimper.

Contents

Contents

Acknowledgements

Brandon would like to thank his wife, Stephanie; daughter, Colbie; and son, Dawson, as well as his parents, Patricia and David, and grandfather William for their continued support, encouragement and direction through a lifetime of researching and experiencing his greatest passions. In addition, special praise and gratitude is extended to coauthor Kristin for the enthusiasm, support, talent and hard work that she poured into this composition full of the things we both find so endearing about a city we love. Lastly, special thanks to the following individuals and families for their support in the production of this body of work: B.L. Strang (photographer), Sherry Bithell (editor), Karl Schwartz (editor), Kate Jenkins (editor, The History Press), David Seidl, the Heath family, the Trimper family, Wayne Bahur, Scott Hudson, Brenda Parker, Monica Thrash, Mark and Donna Altvater, Dean Langrall, Christy Whorton, Jon Christ, Earl Shores, Thomas Kilduffs, Bob Hoffman, Debbi Overly and Gerald Uhlan.

Kristin would like to thank Brandon Seidl, first and foremost, for his talent, support and friendship and for sharing the same niche passion that snowballed first into an online column and finally into an entire book. Thanks also to Karl Schwarz, for his limitless Ocean City knowledge and fact-checking skills; Sherry Bithell, for keeping the copy clean with her eagle eye; Kate Jenkins at The History Press for all of her help and encouragement along the way; Ann McGinnis Hillyer and Anne Neely at OceanCity.com; Joe Kroart and all the good people at Ocean Gallery; Rina Thaler, Katie Brown

ACKNOWLEDGEMENTS

and all the wonderful people at the Art League of Ocean City; Elvis; Dolly Parton; Pip the Beach Cat; Gypsy the Dog; the Life-Saving Station Museum and its dedicated documentarians; Sheila, Mike, Amy and Charlotte Helf; all of the countless people who helped me along on this journey; and finally, my husband and the photographer for this book, B.L. Strang-Moya, thank you for being limitlessly talented and bringing these pages to life and for supporting me along this journey and all others.

And special thanks to Karl Schwartz.

Introduction

"T he ocean stirs the heart, inspires the imagination and brings eternal joy to the soul." American artist Robert Wyland is best known for his murals of marine life, but he's also known for this one apt quote. Anyone who's ever been down to the ocean knows the truth in Wyland's words, and from songs to poems to general musings on the state of human life, there's a proverbial sea of quotes about the ocean because it is just so captivating and vast. The longer we look at it, when we are lucky enough to get down to the ocean and see it in person, the greater it becomes.

Ocean City, Maryland, was once known only for its access to the ocean. In the late nineteenth century, men and women came by railroad and ferry primarily to hunt, fish and comb for seashells. The town was referred to as the "Ladies' Resort to the Ocean," possibly to distinguish it from the rugged accommodations it provided to hunters before it was ever called Ocean City.

First, small cottages, hotels and tackle shops popped up along the shoreline. In the next century and a half, a few cottages weathered storms and remained rooted in town, while others turned into sky-grazing condos and hotels. Some iconic places like the Life-Saving Station Museum and City Hall withstood the test of time and are now historical landmarks in the modern era.

Other things that people remember from their vacations in Ocean City over the decades don't carry as much historical significance but are significant, nonetheless. Ocean City is replete with long-razed mini golf courses and arcades, colorful art installations and hand-carved wooden totem poles, animatronic barkers and antique rides and fiberglass landmarks outside locally famous institutions. These aren't mentioned as often in history books, but they do live on in memories. People look back fondly on their summer vacations in OC and forever associate a barking robotic bulldog, for example, with the sound of arcade games and the smell of salty ocean air.

In a seaside resort town like Ocean City, you can have your historical landmarks and your fiberglass landmarks—and all your other oddities—coexisting peacefully side by side. Sometimes the two overlap. Ocean City, an entire city built around the ocean (which itself is the oldest and probably the oddest oddity in town), is a weird and wonderful place with odd items and sometimes odder people at every turn. That's what makes it so special.

There are plenty of other cities that were built around the ocean, but Ocean City, Maryland, has a special breed of oddness that keeps so many families coming back every summer. So many people look back happily, nostalgically and frequently on their past summer trips "downee ocean, hon."

Everyone's version of what makes something an *oddity* is a little different, and being generous, there's probably far too many "strange or peculiar persons, things or traits," as the word is defined, that two people could begin to cover in one book.

However, Elvis Presley once said—to end with another quote that's not too cheesy this time— "There's no job too immense, when you got confidence." The King himself is an Ocean City oddity in more ways than one. But we'll get to Elvis later.

First, we need to go back to the beginning—not the beginning of the oddness of life and Ocean City but, to make things a little simpler, back to what many consider the beginning of any Ocean City excursion, down on the south side of town where the waves meet the jetty.

Part One
THE INLET

It all starts at the inlet. This is true geographically, as the inlet designates Ocean City's southernmost point and the start of its lively downtown area, and historically, as the inlet is one of the city's largest and most consequential landmarks. It was famously cut through during what's known simply as the Storm of 1933—a major turning point in the town's history and a catalyst for the region's shape and culture as we know it today.

For that reason, our journey begins at the inlet. Our trek through Ocean City will start off a little stormy, pun intended, but once the inlet is formed, it's (mostly) smooth sailing. We'll move among Ocean City's historic haunts and landmarks, through its midtown motels and downtown dives, under the Boardwalk and down by the sea. This journey will visit some of the most famous, and some of the not-as-well-known locales that make Ocean City America's oddest family resort.

Before the Storm of 1933, Ocean City's south end was physically connected to today's Assateague Island, a barrier island located off the east coast of the peninsula that spans parts of Maryland and Virginia. In fact, early plats for Ocean City depicted numbered streets extending about ten blocks south of where the inlet lies today.

Prior to 1933, ocean fishermen had to launch their boats directly from the beach. They had no protected area to dock and were forced to row through the rough line of breaking waves. They also had to haul their catches across the width of Ocean City to the railroad station so they could ship their catches to markets in Baltimore, Philadelphia and New York City. They asked Congress to fund digging a channel between the Atlantic and Coastal Bays—a request that was studied but eventually rejected. On August 22, 1933, Mother Nature answered the fishermen's calls instead.

On that fateful night, businesses and residents in town boarded up and hunkered down. The seas continued to rise, and the winds blew heavy. Waves grew large, and torrential rain continued to fall in sheets, as it had been doing for four days without break, flooding the streets with water, sand and debris. At the peak of the storm, the National Weather Service measured winds of about 150 miles per hour.

When it finally passed and the townspeople emerged from their shelters, they found their homes, businesses and the iconic Boardwalk in shambles, all but completely destroyed. Among the wreckage, they also found that something new had been created: a freshly cut inlet, fifty feet wide and eight feet deep, making a new separation between Ocean City and Assateague Island.

Because the rain had been falling torrentially for four straight days, surrounding bays and their tributaries were flooded and their waters were pushed through the peninsula at Ocean City's lowest and narrowest point. Three streets were washed away permanently and were replaced by the inlet that we know today.

On the fateful storm's seventieth anniversary in 2003, former Ocean City mayor Roland "Fish" Powell recalled watching the water pour across the bay into the ocean. After the storm, crowds of people lined up to gaze in awe at the newly cut natural barrier, he remembered. The barrier continued growing wider and wider as the tides rolled through, carrying with them parts of the old railroad trestle that had been completely washed away.

While the cutting of the inlet would eventually be celebrated as a major win for area fishermen and the town's economy as a whole, the days immediately following the storm were marked by a tone of despair. The town's mayor at the time, William W. McCabe, estimated the damage in the resort to be around $500,000, which, adjusted for inflation, would equate to over $9 million in 2019. Ocean City was battered but not beaten.

The people of Ocean City have always been an industrious and hearty bunch, rising to the occasion time and time again, storm after storm, tide after rising tide. With help from the State of Maryland and the Army Corps of Engineers, the inlet was soon stabilized with two stone jetties on either side, and the ocean was finally permanently accessible from the coastal bays.

The town was rebuilt, except for the old railroad bridge, which would have soon found itself inessential anyway, as the Route 50 bridge (otherwise known by its formal name, the Harry W. Kelley Memorial Bridge) would come to fruition less than a decade later.

Oddly enough, the storm increased the salinity of the Sinepuxent Bay, which resulted in more flavorful oysters and clams. The beach at the south end of the inlet widened to the east when the jetties were installed, and sand moved in to fill the gaps. Tourists continued to flock to Ocean City in droves every summer as they continue to do today. After what could have been a disaster to forever mar the town's history, Ocean City was instead reborn, welcoming a whole host of oddities to be enjoyed by locals and tourists alike for decades to come.

1
Nanticoke, the Whispering Giant

When tourists do migrate to Ocean City, most commonly in the summertime, the inlet is usually the first stop. It's the home of the Hugh T. Cropper Inlet parking lot, the largest parking lot in Ocean City, which is especially well populated on sunny summer days during peak season. Families drive across the Route 50 bridge and head straight for the inlet lot, where their SUVs stay parked all day while they lie out on the beach, weave in and out of downtown shops and traverse the two and one-quarter miles of the famous Ocean City Boardwalk.

Whether they realize it or not, these families—and anyone turning left toward the parking lot when they reach the very end of the mainland and find themselves facing the inlet—are greeted by a twenty-foot landmark that has lived at the inlet boardwalk since 1976. His name is Nanticoke, though he's usually referred to simply as the "Inlet Indian."

Nanticoke was carved by artist Peter Wolf Toth, who spent the latter half of the twentieth century and the beginning of the twenty-first century creating such structures all across the United States. Toth developed a fascination with North American culture, particularly the plight of the Native Americans, at an early age. Originally from Hungary, he and his family fled their homeland in 1956 after the Soviets took over. The family settled in Akron, Ohio, when Toth was still a young boy.

The artist has said he realized his life's purpose when he was just twenty-four years old. He'd briefly studied art at the University of Akron, but when it came to his art, he said, he was largely self-taught. In 1972, he

The totem pole at the inlet was carved by artist Peter Toth and gifted to the people of Maryland in 1976. *B.L. Strang-Moya.*

carved a stone Native American head from a cliff in La Jolla, California, and decided at that moment that he'd continue to carve figures like these for the rest of his life.

After switching mediums from stone to wood and carving another head from a dead elm stump at a park in Akron, Ohio, Toth decided he would carve a wooden sculpture or totem pole to honor Native Americans and give one to each of the fifty states.

The resulting series of sculptures is called the Trail of the Whispering Giants. In the '70s and '80s, Toth traveled to the northern states in the summer and the southern states in the winter in his Dodge maxivan and stayed with whatever local townspeople would have him while he worked on his carvings. He accepted no money for the sculptures but considered them gifts to the country that welcomed his family with open arms back in the 1950s. He provided for himself by working odd jobs, selling his smaller hand-carved trinkets and accepting the generosity of the occasional town or individual who would cover his living expenses while he carved.

The series was completed in May 1988, when Toth finished sculpture No. 58 in Haleiwa, Hawaii. Several states now have more than one sculpture, and there are also several in Canada. Today, Toth lives in Florida, but he still replaces and repairs existing sculptures and carves small ones in his studio.

Nanticoke, who wears a headband with a single feather protruding from the top and who has withstood more than forty years of summer heat, winter frostbite and year-round storms, was the twenty-first sculpture made in the Whispering Giant series. The sculpture depicts a member of the Assateague tribe, a former tribe of the Nanticoke people. The Assateague tribe no longer exists, but the Nanticoke people today are a federal- and state-recognized tribe of Delaware.

Toth carved the sculpture from one-hundred-year-old oak. In 2006, he returned to Ocean City to restore Nanticoke, as the sculpture had weathered decades of storms and heat. Since Hurricane Sandy, which pummeled the East Coast in 2012, and a litany of other storms that have passed through since '06, the sculpture has undergone more damage, and its future in Ocean City is hazy.

Weather inevitably wears wood down after enough time passes, and storms only work to expedite the process; in some regions, Toth's sculptures have deteriorated to the point of falling apart completely and were not replaced. Other towns and cities have restored their sculptures, and in one case, the totem pole was replaced with a fiberglass mold of the original.

Just a short drive north up the Delmarva peninsula lives another Whispering Giant, a twenty-five-foot poplar sculpture located in Bethany Beach, Delaware, standing in the median of Garfield Parkway and Delaware Avenue. That's statue No. 69, which replaced another statue of Toth's that was in decay. The Bethany sculpture is named Chief Little Owl, and in 2002, it was dedicated to Chief Little Owl of the Nanticoke tribe.

Today, Nanticoke and Chief Little Owl just up the way remain standing at their stations tall and proud. Nanticoke continues to overlook the bay, his gaze pointed toward Assateague. He may be weather worn after so many decades standing watch over the Ocean City Inlet, but by now, his presence in Ocean City is about as sure as the ocean's, and there's certainly no one else like him in town.

2
The Life-Saving Station Museum

Nanticoke is lucky enough to see a phenomenal view every day, with his gaze fixed southward past the inlet toward Assateague, a prime spot where many fishermen join him at dusk and dawn to cast their lines and enjoy the view.

What Nanticoke can't see from his current placement is the southern end that most would consider the Boardwalk's starting point, where the Ocean City Life-Saving Station Museum resides. First a home to the local Life-Saving Service, then a post for the U.S. Coast Guard and now an air-conditioned respite for visitors wanting to learn more about local history, the building has seen a lot in its 128-year history.

It would be remiss to not touch on the museum's original purpose as a lifesaving station, which the museum now teaches its visitors about from the moment they step inside. From 1875 until 1915, between the Eastern Shores of Maryland, Delaware and Virginia, it is estimated that 4,500 lives were rescued from sea. Ocean City's Live-Saving Station Museum has plenty of its own stories of rescue and oceanic peril to tell—a captivating history that is portrayed well within the exhibits that encompass the museum's two stories.

The first lifesaving station in the region was built in 1874 at Caroline Street, on land donated by one of Ocean City's founders, Stephen Tabor. It sat alone on the dunes of the Ocean City shore. Because this station was immediately so busy, a new and larger facility was erected in 1891 in the 1882-type architectural style. That building is the one that serves as the

Ocean City's Life-Saving Station Museum is one of approximately 129 remaining stations in the United States. It dates to 1891. *B.L. Strang-Moya.*

museum today. It was an active lifesaving station, used first by the Life-Saving Service and then by the U.S. Coast Guard until 1964.

In 1964, the coast guard abandoned the station for a newer facility on the bay at Worcester Street, and by 1977, the older building was slated for demolition. The Ocean City Museum Society was formed in 1977 to save the historic landmark, and after receiving funding from the mayor and the city council, the old lifesaving station was transported from its spot on the dunes to the Ocean City Inlet, where it remains to this day.

Notably, the space surrounding the museum—the little Boardwalk area that runs parallel to the Inlet Village—is an ode to Eastern Shore maritime history. An old U.S. Coast Guard tower stands a few feet away from the museum and claims the title of oldest observational tower on Maryland's shore. It was erected in 1934 to serve as a lifesaving lookout point and as a watch post for German U-boats during World War II.

Not far from that, and nearly impossible to miss though much closer to the ground, is an ample nineteenth-century anchor that weighs two and a half tons. The anchor was salvaged from an 1870s shipwreck that's known simply as the Sailboat Wreck and was discovered by the commercial clamming vessel *Star Light.*

Above: A sign outside the Life-Saving Station Museum in 1985. While the current Life-Saving Station building was built in 1891, Ocean City's first station was built in 1878. *John Margolies/ Library of Congress.*

Right: The U.S. Coast Guard tower next to the museum was built in 1934 and is the oldest observation tower still standing on Maryland's shore. *John Margolies/Library of Congress.*

Other displays that sit outside the museum, including a pictorial history of the Ocean City Beach Patrol and various shark and marlin replicas, make for a pleasant and educational wandering-through on a mild summer's day.

It's estimated that at one time, nearly 450 lifesaving stations and lifeboat stations existed in the United States, where crewmen responded to shipwrecks and distressed mariners all over the country. Now, Ocean City's lifesaving station is one of approximately 129 original stations still standing, and while some of these stations are still in use by the coast guard, many of them have been abandoned.

"Few other groups of historic American buildings are more endangered than our life-saving and lifeboat stations," states the U.S. Life-Saving Service Heritage Association. "To a far greater extent even than lighthouses, life-saving stations are still being lost and falling into tragic disrepair."

That Ocean City's lifesaving station—not only a landmark but also a piece of living history that educates thousands of visitors every year on the history of Ocean City and the Life-Saving Service—dates to 1891 and stands strong as ever on the inlet boards well over a century later is a testament to the people of Ocean City, who care so deeply about their heritage and the importance of preserving the town's past.

Because of its uniqueness and its historical value, the Life-Saving Station Museum is an oddity—a beautiful, wonderful and educational oddity, much like the host of smaller oddities that exist within its interior walls.

Some of what's inside the museum, too, has great historical value to Ocean City and the United States. And some of what's inside the museum is more of the, well, strange and peculiar variety.

GHOSTS OF THE MUSEUM

The Life-Saving Station Museum is no stranger to apparitional oddities or, at least, assorted claims of them in its century-plus history. The museum's share of ghosts has been covered in books (Mindie Burgoyne's *Haunted Ocean City and Berlin* provides some pretty detailed accounts), in the local news (as seen most recently on 47 ABC's Haunted Delmarva series) and on local ghost tours. Pasadena, Maryland's Dead of Night Paranormal Investigation Team dropped by in 2017 and 2018 and used electronic voice phenomenon (EVP) recorders to "communicate" with the supernatural.

By way of the media and local lore, here are some of the ghost stories that have been passed around.

The Life-Saving Station Museum is modest in size, and almost every inch of its interior is occupied by exhibits. There's not much room for storage inside, so the watch tower outside is used to store miscellaneous museum supplies. Local legend states that once, just a few days after the steps to the watch tower had been repainted, a museum staff member was sent to the tower to retrieve such supplies. No one else had been up the stairs since they'd been painted. The staff member climbed the stairs and, upon reaching the very top, was surprised to see the imprint of a small shoe. There were no marks on the stairs otherwise—just one lone shoeprint. No one working at the museum could offer an explanation.

One of the downstairs exhibits, *Wreck in the Offing*, depicts the history of the Life-Saving Service on the Eastern Shore of Maryland, Delaware and Virginia from 1878 to 1914. Upon entering the exhibit, the first thing a visitor will see is the Life-Car—a small, enclosed vessel made of galvanized iron and painted white, once used in a local rescue mission and now hanging from the museum ceiling. Lifesaving station crewmen would help distressed mariners climb inside the Life-Car and then close its door and pull them to safety through the crashing waves.

A former employee of the museum, Miss Betty, who has since retired, told her ghost story to local travel writer Mindie Burgoyne. A young man and his mother were visiting the museum, Miss Betty said, but they left in a hurry. When the young man came back by himself several months later, he told her that his mother received such a fright in the *Wreck in the Offing* exhibit that she left immediately and vowed to never return. Upon entering the room, she was hit with a rush of cold air. After reading the signage about the Life-Car, she peered into the vessel, which is always empty. But here, where a visitor would normally see a hollow metal interior, the woman claimed to see the body of a drowned sailor. His skin was gray, and he wore a black slicker and a hat. His wet hair was matted to his face. He was certainly dead, the woman said, and covered in seawater, which she said she could smell. The scent mingled eerily with the sound of water dripping from the top of the vessel. She gasped when she saw the sailor. She felt faint, she said. Her son rushed her outside, and her skin was almost freezing when she reached the warm and sunny boardwalk.

It wasn't the first time a mysterious person had appeared in the museum. On another day when Miss Betty and an employee named Richard were closing up at the museum's gift shop entrance, a little boy ran through the front door and made a beeline straight to the exhibits. Miss Betty described the boy as very beautiful and about five years old with blue eyes and blond hair. He was wearing a green shirt. They expected the boy's parents to follow behind him, but no one came. All the doors in the building had already been locked except the front door, but when Richard went to look for the little boy, he was nowhere to be found. The museum was empty. Eventually, Richard and Miss Betty went home, and the boy was never heard from again.

LAFFING SAL AND BRUNO THE BULLDOG

To most visitors of the museum, there's only one object in any of its exhibits that might be spookier than its ghost stories—and she's very, very real, at least physically speaking, in the corporeal realm.

For decades, Laffing Sal was the star feature at Jester's Fun House, one of Ocean City's most memorable twentieth-century amusement attractions, located on Wicomico Street off the Boardwalk. Often misspelled as "Laughing Sal," the large robotic rag doll—the first animatronic of its kind—would shake her head, wave her arms, jerk her torso and laugh while patrons would stop in wonder and inevitably begin laughing along with her.

Sal's early conceptual design and production made her an influencer and forerunner in the amusement industry. She set the pace for a rapid production of animated figures featured around the world in carnivals and amusement parks, including the Disney enterprises. At the height of her popularity, Sal was featured at venues all over the country, but today she can be enjoyed at only a handful of remaining attractions.

Mr. Jester purchased Laffing Sal in the early 1940s for about $360 (around $6,500 today) from the Philadelphia Toboggan Company (PTC) based in Germantown, Pennsylvania. When she arrived, she was placed in front of the Fun House to greet guests and, in later years, exhibited behind a chicken wire cage to prevent passersby from reaching for her, often resulting in vandalism. Buttons to make her work were wired to a nearby concession stand, where the Jesters were able to control her every move at a moment's notice.

Laffing Sal as she appears today in the Life-Saving Station Museum. *B.L. Strang-Moya.*

Standing over six feet tall, Sal had a simple internal makeup of papier-mâché and pressed card stock mounted on a steel frame comprised of numerous coils. Beneath her famous dress, the interior construction was rudimentary, consisting of pins, staples, nails and nuts and bolts, as all of her extremities were detachable for simpler shipping and storage. Visible to the public, the laughing lady donned a bright pink dress, a handbag, large Mary Jane shoes and a big floppy hat. It's rumored that the PTC did not originally produce hats for the Sals, and they were to be supplied by the buyer, although original ads depicted the display complete with a hat.

Sal's famous laugh track was originally transmitted by a 78-rpm record player concealed beneath her pedestal, which measured twelve inches in diameter. It wasn't until the record stopped that the lucky attraction operator that day would have to restart the record—a cycle that would typically last only a few minutes. The invention of tapes would eventually automate that task. Interestingly, and according to legend, the voice talent

Above: Laffing Sal as she appears today. *B.L. Strang-Moya.*

Left: Laffing Sal advertisement from the Philadelphia Toboggan Company as featured in the October 10, 1942 issue of the *Billboard* magazine. *Authors' collections.*

that performed the famous Sal laugh was not that of a lady but that of an intoxicated gentleman.

Jester's Fun House was built in 1927 by Thomas Conway of Atlantic City, New Jersey. Conway, who also owned several other small businesses, managed it for only four years before selling it to Lloyd Jester, due to his own poor health. The attraction had a large façade, with the words "Fun House" clearly displayed on both the front and the roofline. Along with images depicting clowns and ballyhoo, the interior featured effects such as air bags, floor obstacles, a tilt room, dancing skeletons, a stunt titled "Bruno" (a bulldog that suddenly sprang out at unsuspected patrons), a large gorilla and even an octopus.

In 1970, Mr. Jester retired from the fun house business and turned it over to his son, Lloyd Jester Jr. The fun house was demolished after only two years under his son. It made room for Sportland, also owned by the Jester family. After the fun house's closing, Sal was transported to a storage facility in Berlin, where she was later vandalized, resulting in her face being disfigured and her garment left knackered.

Laffing Sal and Bruno the Bulldog were two of the only stunts retained from the attraction. Sal was donated to the Ocean City Life-Saving Station Museum in the summer of 1980 by Mrs. Jester and was restored soon after.

Bruno the Bulldog, an original staple attraction at Jester's Fun House, can still be seen today in the Life-Saving Station Museum. *Brandon Seidl.*

Now she can be seen and heard on the second floor of the museum in the boardwalk exhibit. With only the push of a button, Sal will laugh as she did for generations on Ocean City's Boardwalk. Unfortunately, her movements have long been defunct.

A lot of paranormal activity has been associated with the old Ocean City Sal. Workers have reported hearing her laugh after closing time with no explanation. Sal was originally featured at venues all over the country and can still be enjoyed at more than thirty venues today.

3

The Fishing Pier

P erhaps the most symbolic landmark of Ocean City's south end is the famous fishing pier, which was first opened to the public in July 1907, after three years of often onerous construction. Visitors and locals alike would be hard-pressed to find a piece of Ocean City literature without a photo or mention of the pier, which extends 489 feet into the Atlantic, often accompanied by Jolly Roger's towering Ferris wheel added in 1986 and a skyline featuring various other amusements and buildings.

Thanks to a unique vision and ambitious local investors of the early twentieth century, along with talented builders and promoters, the pier has morphed from a once-gratifying hub of fishing and trapshooting activities for families in the olden days to a beautiful backdrop for photo ops and sightseeing for today's generations.

Throughout the pier's history as "watch-dog" over the heart of the town, it has endured many cases of adversity, including countless misfortunes from Mother Nature and fire. On more than one occasion, harsh winters and chunks of ice built up in the ocean severely damaged the structure, eventually leading to a shortening of its overall length by 140 feet in 1978.

Many coastal storms and hurricanes have repeatedly and relentlessly pummeled and thus eliminated the easternmost portion of the pier—one recent culprit being Hurricane Sandy in 2012—resulting in costly rebuilds. But perhaps the most devastating event was the Great Boardwalk Fire of December 1925, which destroyed the pier, the Pier Building, two of Ocean

Ocean City's famous amusement pier and ride lineup in 2004. *Courtesy of H. Michael Heath.*

The fishing pier extending out into the Atlantic. Stopping in the Bait & Tackle shop at the pier's entrance for a snack or souvenir is a favorite pastime for many. *B.L. Strang-Moya.*

City's first hotels (the Atlantic and the Seaside) and numerous concessions and amusements.

By 1929, a new seven-hundred-foot pier was constructed by the Sinepuxent Pier and Improvement Company. Although the overall structure has changed in scope and appearance through the years, it continues to thrive in many different capacities.

Synonymous with the pier itself is the building that fronts its entrance, which has been offering entertainment to young and old since construction of the original pavilion was complete in 1907. The building as it stands today was erected in 1926 and is in the same location as the original pavilion structure, which was destroyed by the December 24, 1925 fire.

The two-story venue is a nine-bay-by-five-bay rectangular building that hosted ballroom dancing and big-band music in its early years. Since then, it has hosted many commercial and entertainment ventures, including bowling alleys, billiard tables, a movie theater, a convention hall, a teen center and, more recently, a wax museum, a laser tag arena and a few renditions of the Ripley's Believe it or Not museum.

Today, the pier and its complementary buildings remain successful staples of the amusement district in the downtown area. Jolly Roger Amusement Park occupies the pier under the management of its owner, Charles "Buddy" Jenkins, who continues to be at the forefront of the city's amusement market since he opened his first venue, a miniature golf course, in 1964. Jenkins's vast collection of rides, amusements, games and concessions remains a highlight for Boardwalk visitors and those who venture over the Atlantic on Ocean City's iconic promenade.

MORBID MANOR (R.I.P.)

One of Ocean City's most iconic old amusements that lived on the pier in the later part of the twentieth century is Morbid Manor. Not to be confused with the Ocean City Haunted House dark ride, Morbid Manor was a staple of the pier that terrorized kids for two decades.

Debuting for its first season in 1975, the manor was a two-and-a-half-story walk-through attraction made famous by its live actors, demonizing appearance, sinister sounds and effects and Victorian-style façade with faux-neglected exterior gardens. In short, the attraction's artistry and details made visitors believe that an actual abandoned house had been uprooted and placed on the pier.

The sinister façade of Morbid Manor as it appeared on the pier in 1991. *Courtesy of Robert Hoffman.*

Towering over the pier and recognizable from virtually any distance on the Boardwalk, it provided a rather supernatural experience that scared hundreds of thousands of brave patrons during its twenty-year tenure on the boards. Perhaps most memorable was the tail of an airplane sticking out of the building's top-floor window, and guests from the late 1980s may recall the attraction operating under the name "Year of the Vampire" for a brief time.

The manor was designed and constructed by legendary dark ride designer Fred Mahana, who is known for his groundbreaking work in Wildwood, New Jersey, on attractions such as Hitchcock Manor, Dracula's Castle and Theater of Blood. Mahana had a knack for making any concept a reality, despite how far-fetched it may have initially seemed. At the start of the Morbid Manor's life span, the pier was under the ownership and management of Ocean Amusements Inc.

One of the scariest elements of the attraction was the talented live actors who strategically hid in the manor and chased customers with chainsaws. At times, the actors were theater majors from colleges and universities who came to work at the attraction for the summer. Their makeup and costumes altered their appearance just enough to leave even the bravest visitor screaming in terror.

Unknown to many, the manor was a hip place in off hours. The management and workers of the ride would often hold band practices and other activities behind closed doors. They also slept there throughout the nights, despite a lack of air conditioning and uncomfortable one-hundred-degree summer temperatures. To those who ran the attraction, it was more than a job—it was life. Former employees of the attraction still share their

Morbid Manor amid a robust ride lineup on the pier in 1983. *Courtesy of Gerald Uhlan.*

A young man poses just south of the pier building in front of the iconic Morbid Manor sign in 1976. *Courtesy of Gerald Uhlan.*

Left: A carnival game sits beside the Morbid Manor in 1985. *John Margolies/Library of Congress.*

Below: A curious young lady surveys the damage after a fire destroyed the Morbid Manor in November 1995. *Courtesy of Christy Whorton.*

stories and pride for the attraction that was basically a second home for many years.

In early November 1995, a real-life horror show transpired on the pier when Morbid Manor burned to the ground. Fire crews from Ocean City, Ocean Pines and Berlin worked tirelessly to fight the fire but were unable to salvage the famous attraction. Ironically, the ride had just undergone a large renovation the year before and both the interior and exterior had been completely revamped. Although the building had a complete sprinkler system, it was reportedly shut down for the winter to prevent the pipes from freezing.

Shortly after the devastating fire, rumors began to circulate regarding the cause of the blaze. Some believe it was an electrical fire, while others believe it was caused by sparks from the grinding and cutting of steel for the removal of a nearby waterslide. Firefighters completed an investigation and concluded that the fire did not seem suspicious, although a final cause was never publicized.

After the manor was destroyed by fire, an effort was made to keep the dark ride tradition alive on the pier by adding a portable dark ride called Ghost in the late 1990s. Ghost was a Barbisan dark ride from Italy that included several animated stunts and a façade that resembled a castle. After several years of operation, Ghost was renamed Ghost Pirates, and artists added pirate and nautical imagery to the façade. It was completely removed in 2006.

The next season, a Zachini portable dark ride was added, this time called Morbid Manor II. The ride featured mostly metal sculptures for effects and included very few animatronics. In 2010, the ride was overhauled with a 3D façade. New props were added, and the ride was renamed Morbid Manor 3D, in an effort to attract a broader audience. The ride lives on as Morbid Manor Motel with a zombie twist.

THE WAX MUSEUM

Briefly overlapping with Morbid Manor's tenure on the pier was the Wax Museum, a relic of '90s Ocean City that lived on the pier for just four years during the 1992 through 1995 seasons. Even with its brief life span, the Wax Museum is remembered fondly by those who were able to stop in and see the waxy likenesses of stars, including Elvis Presley and Marilyn Monroe.

Left: An eye-catching billboard spanning the width of the pier building advertises the new Wax Museum in 1992. *Courtesy of Debbi Overly.*

Below: A brochure promotes the new Wax Museum and its "Seven Wondrous Worlds in Wax," which included more than 150 lifelike figures. *Authors' collections.*

Ocean City's Exciting

WAX MUSEUM

MARILYN MONROE

LARGEST MUSEUM On the East Coast
OVER 150 LIFELIKE FIGURES
FUN FOR THE ENTIRE FAMILY

Pier Building
Boardwalk at
Wicomico Street
Ocean City, MD
410-289-7766

$1.00 Off Admission
For your entire party
WAX MUSEUM
NOT GOOD WITH
OTHER DISCOUNTS
EXP. 12/31/92

OCEAN CITY
WAX MUSEUM

SEVEN WONDROUS WORLDS IN WAX

THE WORLD OF STARS
Charlie Chaplin - Marcel Marceau
Clint Eastwood - Barbra Streisand
John Wayne - Sammy Davis Jr.
Burt Reynolds - Lucille Ball
Marilyn Monroe - Diana Ross
And many, many more. . .

THE WORLD OF MUSIC
Dolly Parton - Johnny Cash - Elvis!
Willie Nelson - Michael! - Hank Williams
Louis Armstrong - Minnie Pearl
And many, much more. . .

THE WORLD OF MOVIELAND
Fred Astaire and Ginger Rogers
Clark Gable and Vivian Leigh in "Gone With The Wind"
Yul Brynner in "The King and I"
Richard Burton and Elizabeth Taylor in "Taming Of The Shrew"
Humphrey Bogart in "Casablanca"
And much, much more. . .

THE WORLD OF DISCOVERY
The Great California Gold Rush
The Wright Brothers at Kitty Hawk
Louis Pasteur - Thomas Edison - Madame Curie
Neil Armstrong's Walk On The Moon
And much, much more. . .

THE WORLD OF MAKE BELIEVE
Hansel and Gretel - Sleeping Beauty
Pinocchio and Gepetto - Cinderella
Tom Sawyer and Huckleberry Finn
Tales of Hans Christian Anderson
And much, much more. . .

THE WORLD OF COURAGE-FINALE
The Greek Chariot Wars - Lady Godiva
Rides Thru Coventry
Francis Scott Key Gives Birth To Our National Anthem
And much, much more. . .

THE WORLD OF THE HORRIBLE
Frankenstein - Wolfman - Dracula - Mummyman
Phantom of the Opera - Hunchback of Notre Dame
Aztec Sacrifice - Voodoo Magic - Burning Witches
Snake Victim - Rat Torture - Water Torture - Spikes Victim
And many, many more. . .

DOWNTOWN OCEAN CITY

RT. 50   WAX MUSEUM
PHILADELPHIA
BALTIMORE
WICOMICO
BOARDWALK
FISHING PIER
MUNICIPAL PARKING LOT
INLET

OPEN 10 A.M. - 12 MIDNIGHT IN SEASON

GROUP RATES

OPEN YEAR ROUND

The museum was developed and operated by C.M. Uberman Enterprises out of Gettysburg, Pennsylvania, and included more than 150 lifelike figures displayed in "Seven Wondrous Worlds in Wax." Such iconic figures as Willie Nelson, Superman, Groucho Marx, Frank Sinatra and Michael Jackson were featured in the museum's dark, winding hallways. Many of the wax figures in the museum were manufactured by Henry Alvarez of Alvarez Wax Models in Long Beach, California, and were created with secret sculpting and painting methods passed down by his mentors.

The themed areas of the museum included the World of Stars, the World of Music, the World of Movieland, the World of Discovery, the World of Make Believe, the World of Courage and the World of the Horrible. Each display was often accompanied by rich sound effects and lighting.

In September 1995, it was officially announced that the Ocean City Wax Museum, which opened its doors in 1992 in the Pier Building, would close its doors forever. When the museum first opened, it claimed to be the largest wax museum on the East Coast.

After the Ocean City Wax Museum closed, the wax figures were auctioned off one by one to both commercial operations and private collectors all over the country. Although the museum left indelible memories on so many—most notably the large painted mural on the outside wall that featured Frankenstein's monster—information about the attraction remains rather ellusive given its short-lived time on the Boardwalk.

Part Two

THE BOARDWALK

In wintertime, the Boardwalk is a place of respite. Bundle up, and it's perfect for peaceful strolls along the beach. The sound of the ocean and the seagull's caw, along with a look at the shimmering Atlantic Ocean, are just a few of the magical, restorative qualities that keep visitors coming back even in the dead of winter.

In summertime, it comes alive. The wooden boards feel the footsteps of millions of excited visitors eager to take in all the amusements, the shops and the famous Boardwalk snacks, which work together to produce a carefree feeling that's second to none. The peace of the winter boards is replaced by the happy chaos of the summer crowds, and that's just fine.

A coastal beach town is only as good as its boardwalk, and Ocean City's two-and-a-quarter-mile thruway that spans from the inlet in the south up to Twenty-Seventh Street and the start of "Motel Row" midtown is as good as it gets.

It wasn't always three miles long, and in Ocean City's earliest years, it wasn't there at all. It wasn't until the very early twentieth century that owners of beachfront hotels in the still-

Looking south on the Boardwalk in 1985. *John Margolies/Library of Congress.*

developing resort teamed up to construct a wooden walkway that would make traveling between the businesses on the sand much easier and more convenient for guests.

The boards were a temporary fixture. When the tide rose, business owners rolled them up and stored them on their front porches. Almost ten years later, in 1910, a more permanent walkway that spanned five blocks was constructed. In the 1920s, the Boardwalk was extended to Fifteenth Street, and when it had to be totally rebuilt after the Ash Wednesday Storm of '62, it was extended all the way to Twenty-Seventh Street, where it ends today.

After more than a century of life and nearly three miles that cover Ocean City's most frequented and arguably most iconic region, there's a lot of history that those boards have witnessed firsthand. If wooden planks could talk, these could fill anthologies with all they've seen over the years.

The inlet is synonymous with the south end of the Ocean City Boardwalk, but to break our oddities into more bite-size chunks, we've separated them into two individual regions. In truth, you can't separate the modern inlet region from the boards any more than you can separate a surfer from the Atlantic's crashing waves. Here, starting at the south end of the Boardwalk next to the Inlet Village shops and the Inlet Lodge and parallel to the Ocean City Life-Saving Station Museum, our Boardwalk journey begins.

4
Trimper's Rides and Amusements

Essentially, from the resort's very start, Ocean City has been known for its wide-ranging array of amusements. Dating to 1891, it has been home to dozens of amusement parks and venues. Some have withstood the test of time and are still in operation today, while others entertained the young and old for only a few seasons.

One park that has withstood the test of time is Trimper's Rides and Amusements, which starts at the Boardwalk and ventures west out onto the blacktop pavement lots downtown.

Trimper's is the oldest operating family-owned amusement park in the United States, and many consider it the oldest family-owned park in the world. (To some, Trimper's ranks second to England's Blackgang Chine, but according to amusement park historian Jim Futrell, Blackgang Chine wasn't really an amusement park until after Trimper's was established.)

Trimper's celebrated its 125th anniversary in the summer of 2018 with a ribbon-cutting ceremony in its historical merry-go-round building in the presence of multiple public officials and dignitaries.

"The year was 1893," Trimper's vice president Stephanie Trimper Lewis said at the ceremony. "Grover Cleveland was being sworn in as our twenty-fourth president. Thomas Edison was finishing another invention and constructing the first motion picture studio. The new invention at the World's Fair was the first Ferris wheel ride—that's appropriate. And down here in Ocean City, my great-grandparents, Dan and Margaret Trimper, opened up two hotels along the beach."

Trimper's Rides is lit on a hot summer night in July 1999. *Brandon Seidl.*

Her great-grandparents had visited Ocean City several years prior to their move. When they went home to Baltimore, they closed their catering business and sold their bar, the Silver Dollar Saloon. They opened two hotels on the Boardwalk, the Eastern Shore and the Sea Bright. But Daniel Trimper wasn't content just being a hotelier. His passion was for entertainment and amusements.

It wasn't long before, in the outdoor pavilion of the Sea Bright Hotel, the Trimpers started offering live theater, boxing matches, gambling, billiards, a bar, dancing, a shooting gallery, a roller rink, a live alligator exhibit and the carousel that still goes around in the amusement park today.

"I can only imagine how delighted he would be 125 years later to see how his vision has grown," Lewis said.

The modern rendition of Trimper's Rides offers a unique but traditional experience featuring newer state-of-the-art rides and attractions while continuing to operate vintage antique classics from yesteryear. It has always been a blacktop pavement park with portable rides trucked in each season, but it's also home to many historic buildings, such as the Inlet Lodge and other structures that date back nearly a century. While the seaside park has weathered hundreds of storms, a changing market and challenging financial times, it has proven to be resilient during the most adverse conditions and continues to delight those who visit.

THE HERSCHELL-SPILLMAN CAROUSEL

There are several classic rides at Trimper's to note, but the most breathtaking is the original 1912 menagerie carousel built by the Herschell-Spillman Company in New York. Initially run by a steam engine, the fifty-foot-diameter carousel features three rows, two levels, four chariots and forty-eight hand-carved animals, twenty-three of which are horses. Multiple other

Trimper's famous Menagerie Carousel built by the Herschell-Spillman Company, prior to its multiyear restoration in the early 1970s. *Trimper's Rides Archive.*

The "Forever Joanne" carousel horse, named in honor of Joanne Trimper, who passed away in 1991. Joanne was the wife of the late Granville Trimper. *Brandon Seidl.*

antique rides, such as the Fairy Whip, water boats, airplanes, Hamptons and the dodgem bumper cars round out the inside of the building.

Trimper's carousel is one of the oldest continually operating carousels in the United States. Some allege that it's haunted by Joanne Trimper, the wife of Granville D. Trimper. Granville ran the park's operations until his death in 2008. It's rumored that Joanne's signature perfume will sometimes waft by as the carousel makes its rotations. The carousel was Joanne's favorite ride, and the scent of her perfume is said to be especially strong near her favorite horse, a white steed adorned with red roses, a turquoise sash and a beige saddle. The horse was named "Forever Joanne" in her honor after she passed away.

BONANZA SHOOTING GALLERY

The north side of Trimper's carousel building near the South Division Street entrance is home to the family's famous 1970s-era bonanza shooting gallery, manufactured by the Taylor Engineering Corporation out of California.

These types of galleries first made their debut in the amusement industry in the late 1950s, and within twenty-five years, their locations dotted the country. The layout of the Trimper gallery was standard then, and the majority of the Bonanza "Old West" galleries that parks installed looked nearly identical. The Trimpers still operate the game

Trimper's Bonanza Shooting Gallery as it appeared in 2008. *Brandon Seidl.*

The gallery's famous pianist waits to play your favorite old-fashioned tune. *Brandon Seidl.*

using mostly original electronics, although the photocell sensors to trigger the gallery's air-operated animation and antics were replaced with LED targets in 2010.

The most popular target in the gallery is the outlandish Piano Man, who has been playing the same tune and wearing the same knackered attire for nearly half a century. Other targets include various animal critters, beer cans, lights, skulls and even a sewing machine and cuckoo clock. Counter lengths and the number of shooting stations varied from park to park depending on available space, but the Trimpers have proudly maintained a notable fifteen shooting stations and approximately eighty unique targets in the gallery since its inception.

ALADDIN'S LAMP

Collectively, more than one hundred rides, games, concessions and attractions are offered at Trimper's Rides. But with a consistent change in visitor interest and an increased cost to maintain rides at the highest

Aladdin's Lamp Fun House as it appeared in 1999 after a façade refurbishment. *Brandon Seidl.*

and safest level, sometimes memory-makers are forced to fade to just that: a memory. At the end of the 2017 season, one of the park's most iconic fun houses, Aladdin's Lamp (Salem Aleikum), was permanently retired. The decision was made due to increased costs to maintain and reduced ridership.

For generations, the colorful Arabian nights–themed fun house stood tall in the back of Trimper's Rides and Amusements, while the iconic genie bowed his head from his seat atop the ride's entrance. The attraction first appeared at Trimper's Rides in the mid-1970s and is often remembered for its unique floor challenges, ramps, spinning tunnels, mazes and psychedelic rooms—not to mention its darkness. Riders were not allowed on the attraction with open-toed shoes as a safety precaution, and visitors would have the option of walking through the "chicken exit" if they were apprehensive about their balance capabilities in the spinning tunnel. The attraction's roof, made of canvas, provided a memorable smell that visitors looked forward to year after year. Now, all of these experiences are relived only in memories.

The Salem Aleikum fun house series was the brainchild of German amusement designer Willi Schafer, and the Aladdin's Lamp attraction made its debut in 1972 at a carnival in Cologne, Germany. Many identified Schafer as an amusement industry leader. An advertisement from 1971 depicts the new Salem Aleikum as featuring "many amusement effects under one roof," which indeed it did. Its massive façade was one to behold, with a front that measured ninety feet wide, thirty-nine feet deep and forty-two feet tall.

Schafer would later design attractions that French amusement company Reverchon would manufacture and sell. Coincidentally, Reverchon was also the manufacturer of Trimper's Himalaya ride, which, as of this writing, remains in operation adjacent to where Aladdin's Lamp stood. (Even if the Himalaya spins a bit too fast for one's liking, the retro ski-slope mural design that decorates the ride's exterior and wraps into its interior portion makes it well worth a walk-by.)

Before long, a Swiss showman named Edy Meier premiered a Salem Aleikum attraction in the United States on Casino Pier of Seaside Heights, New Jersey. Supposedly, that attraction was lost in 1976 due to storm damage from Hurricane Belle. Information about the origin of Trimper's Aladdin's Lamp remains largely a mystery, although it's certain that Granville Trimper negotiated its acquisition.

The attraction's famous Genie towers over the entrance ready to grant you a wish. *Brandon Seidl.*

Aladdin's Lamp as it appeared in 2013, after an overhaul to reduce its footprint and allow more room for various attractions nearby. *Brandon Seidl.*

Tom Lokey of Baltimore, who worked at Trimper's Rides and ran the now-defunct Wild Mouse roller coaster, remembers helping unload sea containers from France that transported the attraction in the mid-1970s. In fact, he chipped a tooth that day when a piece of the ride went astray, and he still has that chip to this day. Despite the ride being only a few years old when it landed permanently at Trimper's, it's likely that it traveled the carnival circuit in Germany before it arrived in the United States.

The attraction's most recent overhaul was in 2013, when its footprint was reduced by nearly half to allow room for other attractions nearby. Despite a smaller floor plan, the Trimpers managed to retain all of the original floor traps and stunts and incorporate them into the new design. Routine refurbishment and painting of the exterior and interior took place every few years during the off-season to keep the attraction in tip-top shape. The sister attraction to Aladdin's Lamp, Grand Orient, is still in operation at Palace Playland in Old Orchard Beach, Maine, as of this writing.

PIRATES COVE

Aladdin's Lamp may be lost to the sands of time, but there's still one extravagant vintage fun house that remains open for business on Trimper's grounds. The Pirates Cove dates to 1971, when Granville Trimper commissioned Bill Tracy to begin work on the attraction after he decided it was time to add a fun house to his growing collection of amusements. A concrete building forty-five feet wide and thirty-seven feet deep was constructed to house the attraction on the back side of the park near its entrance.

Right: The façade of the Pirates Cove at Trimper's Rides as it appeared in 1971, shortly after construction. *Trimper's Rides Archive.*

Below: One of the most popular Bill Tracy stunts is the Ghost Pilot, a skeleton pirate turning the ship's wheel on the stern of a ghost ship. *Brandon Seidl.*

Ahoy! The attraction's iconic pirate, refurbished in 2016 and built primarily of fiberglass, keeps a close eye on park visitors near and far. *Brandon Seidl.*

Tracy didn't miss a trick in this old-fashioned fun house. The lobby area is full of floor obstacles, such as a drawbridge and moving ship deck. Inside, visitors encounter forced-perspective hallways, a spinning tunnel, a mirror maze with strobe lighting and nearly twenty original stunts. No one can miss the exterior façade, which towers over the rest of the park, thanks to Tracy's maritime theming and iconic "parade float" pirate figure, which was completely refurbished in 2016. By the early '90s, Trimper had commissioned the Sally Corporation in Jacksonville, Florida, to custom manufacture an attention-grabbing animated show consisting of bantering parrots for the attraction's façade.

The side of the building, although exposed to the public, is covered with ten-foot fiberglass stone panels that feature the distinct heads of skeleton pirates, and a lone crew member twenty-four feet in the air in the crow's nest can be seen at the park's entrance. None of the original eighteen stunts has been removed from the attraction, although over the years, the Trimpers have added new effects and lighting. The façade underwent a full-scale renovation in the spring of 2019, and thanks to the Trimper family, it remains one of the most complete Tracy fun houses left in America.

TRIMPER'S HAUNTED HOUSE

Trimper's Haunted House, a true national amusement oddity, was built in 1964 by legendary dark ride designer Bill Tracy—designer of Pirates Cove and countless other fun houses and dark rides—on the site of the former Windsor Theater. Originally built as a one-story attraction with a fleet of eight cars, the ride was leveled and rebuilt as a two-story ride in 1988, using the remnants of another Tracy attraction, the Ghost Ship, acquired by Granville Trimper from the defunct Ocean Playland Amusement Park on Sixty-Fifth Street. (More on that later.)

Visitors venture through the attraction in a vessel modeled on an antique coffin, complete with "Rest in Peace" etched on the back. The coffin pushes its way through creaking double doors into the darkness of the haunted house, and riders find themselves disoriented in crooked passageways, turned inside-out as they're forced through a spinning vortex, suddenly upside-down in one of the mansion's bedrooms, frightened as they come face-to-face with an oncoming locomotive and always either terrified or amused by Bill Tracy's unforgettable stunts.

Left: Trimper's Haunted House as it appeared in August 1967. *Courtesy of Earl Shores.*

Below: Bill Tracy's demonic bat dominantly displayed on the ride's spooky façade each summer. *Brandon Seidl.*

Such classic papier-mâché Tracy stunts as the Knit Wit, Old Mill, Torture Chamber, Swamp Ghost, Last Drop and Cuckoo Clock can be found in this one-of-a-kind seaside treasure. In all, there are more than twenty original stunts remaining in the attraction, making it one of the most "True to Tracy" dark rides left in existence. For those who enjoy modernized horror effects, the ride also includes an amplitude of newer and more modern stunts and props. The ride lasts only five minutes, prompting many visitors to ride it again and again—or at least once every summer.

In addition to Tracy's host of Day-Glo papier-mâché oddities inside the haunted house, the gum door, which is really two double doors that lead

Right: Count Wolf von Vinderstein, the famous animatronic lobby barker installed in 1995, was built by the Sally Corporation out of Jacksonville, Florida. Granville Trimper negotiated a deal on the spot and purchased the model as we see it today right off the showroom floor at the 1994 International Association of Amusement Parks and Attractions convention. *Brandon Seidl.*

Below: The Birthday Party, one of Tracy's most bizarre and demented creations, came from Ocean Playland's Ghost Ship and was installed in 1989. *Brandon Seidl.*

The Last Drop, the mansion's bathroom scene, screams of Bill Tracy's sense of humor. A helpless victim screams for help as he's flushed down the toilet. *Brandon Seidl.*

Brandon poses with Bill Tracy's 1964 Attic Rat stunt, as seen in the first room of Trimper's Haunted House. *Brandon Seidl.*

The façade of Trimper's Haunted House as it appeared in 2017, after undergoing a full refurbishment the year before. *Brandon Seidl.*

back inside from the second-story balcony, is plenty odd itself. At some point in the early history of the ride's second story, riders started sticking their used chewing gum onto the sides of the doors, and while the Trimpers staff keeps the ride excellently maintained, it's not uncommon to find dozens of pieces of chewed-up gum in every shade of the rainbow stuck to those creaking double doors. Spooky.

LANDMARK CHARACTERS: BILL TRACY

Often referred to as a man of great mystery, Bill Tracy has affected all of us in various ways through the past sixty-plus years, whether we know it or not. A pioneer in the amusement industry and creator of the aforementioned Trimper's Haunted House and Pirates Cove rides, Tracy's vision and innovation helped define the model for what dark rides and fun houses should be. Many of his ideas and concepts are still widely used today. As he completed projects in parks up and down the East Coast in the 1960s and early 1970s, we've all most certainly seen or experienced his works of art at least once.

Bill Tracy featured with Swamp Ghost in an *Amusement Business* advertisement from late December 1961. *Courtesy of the Bill Tracy Project Collection.*

Bill Tracy in one of his unique advertisements published in the March 24, 1962 issue of *Amusement Business. Courtesy of the Bill Tracy Project Collection.*

Tracy's professional career started in 1952, when he began working as a designer and builder of outdoor amusement displays. From 1952 to 1954, he served as the art director for Ringling Bros. and Barnum & Bailey Circus in Sarasota, Florida, where he created spectacular floats, props and costumes and became nationally known for his creative efforts. In 1953, Macy's department store contracted Tracy to design and build window displays and floats for the Macy's Thanksgiving Day Parade in New York City.

During the late 1950s, a transition took place that changed Tracy's focus and the amusement park industry forever. His inner "dark side" took over, and he went from creating happy, appealing and eye-catching window displays, parade floats and circus props to creating the most horrific, disturbing, provocative and controversial dark ride displays the amusement park industry had ever seen.

Bill Tracy's journey into the dark ride industry began when he was contracted as a freelance artist for established dark ride manufacturers, including the famous Pretzel Amusement Ride Company. Tracy developed the façades and stunts for Pretzel-built rides, including the Orient Express at Million Dollar Pier in Atlantic City, New Jersey, before he decided to venture out on his own. By the early 1960s, Tracy had found his niche, and the final phase of his illustrious professional career was well underway.

When Tracy designed a dark ride, it would consist of an elaborate façade, interior stunts and props and a ride system to carry visitors through the alternate world that he created. He believed that the façade of a dark ride was just as important as what was inside it. The façade serves as the marketing and advertisement for the ride, and it aims to lure people to use some of their precious ride tickets on that particular attraction. This design strategy was clearly apparent, as no other dark ride designer of the era developed such decorative and complex façades as Tracy.

Bill Tracy's Tilted Corridor, original to the ride's 1964 installation, uses forced perspective, ultraviolet lighting, painted murals and dimensional timbers to offer riders a sense of unreality. *Brandon Seidl.*

The interior stunts of this era, the early to mid-1960s, were more complex mechanically than in later years. During this time, most of the stunts were triggered "events," such as a female victim being cut in half by a large circular saw. These stunts had complex mechanical systems to achieve the animation, Amuse-pak sound cartridge repeaters to create the sounds and timed lighting to bring the stunts out from the darkness.

All of these mechanical systems had to be custom fabricated for each stunt, and they also had to be discreet, so they wouldn't take away from the ingenious artistry of the stunt itself. They also had to be dependable to minimize maintenance requirements, as they operated through thousands of cycles a month. Many of Tracy's original mechanical concepts continued operating dependably for decades.

Manfred Bass, one of the first sculptors Tracy hired, recalled that the title of the company's catalogue, *We Work in the Dark*, was a reference to the motto of his fluorescent workshop. The Tracy gang actually did work in the dark when painting stunts and props so they could be sure that the final product was seen in the proper environment under ultraviolet lights. In

Bill Tracy dominates on the cover of his 1962 catalogue titled *We Work in the Dark* under his company Outdoor Dimensional Display Co. Inc. *Courtesy of the Bill Tracy Project Collection.*

1962, an average stunt cost $1,500, and a complete two-story package dark ride cost approximately $40,000 ($325,000 today) in addition to the cost of the building structure itself. On average, a dark attraction took only a few weeks to install once the building was constructed.

One of Tracy's biggest accomplishments was the design and construction of Trimper's Haunted House on the Ocean City Boardwalk. By January 1964, Granville Trimper and Bill Tracy were having regular phone calls to discuss overview, cost, site visits and plans for what would become Trimper's Haunted House. Tracy's first visit to Ocean City was on January 21, 1964, when he met with Granville to scope the possible location and specifications for the ride at the site of the former Windsor Theater.

Tracy built a scale model of the ride for Granville to review by February, and by April, a contract between Bill Tracy and Granville Trimper was signed. Construction would take place during the early summer months, and the attraction would open to the public by midsummer of 1964.

Tracy produced fewer rides in the early 1970s and experienced some financially disappointing years. His last known project was Whacky Shack at

Joyland Amusement Park in Wichita, Kansas, which opened in 1974, shortly before his death in August of that year. Most would say that Trimper's Haunted House was one of Tracy's most successful flagship projects, but he'll be remembered for more than eighty other projects around the country, including forty-two dark rides, twelve walk-throughs, nine water rides and many more ride displays, concepts, designs and layouts.

Special thanks to Wayne Bahur for his research and insight into the life and work of Bill Tracy.

THE INLET LODGE

Every town has its own cache of secrets. Ocean City, as you might have noticed, is no different. The Trimper family holds claim to one of the best-kept secrets in town—the Inlet Lodge, hidden in plain sight on the south end of the Boardwalk.

The Inlet Lodge operates beside all the lustrous and loud rides the family business has amassed over the decades that send kids screaming into the air while hard rock radio blasts into the crowd. It's only steps away from the place where a headless barker beckons passersby into a neon-painted, giant bat–guarded Haunted House and where employees yell into microphones and entice kids to games of whack-a-mole with giant plush prizes. Thrown into the summertime chaos of the Boardwalk, it's easy to miss the Inlet Lodge and its first-floor bar, both of which are perfectly welcoming and charming but neither of which do much to draw attention to themselves.

The Inlet Lodge was built on a plot acquired by Granville C. Trimper in 1945. The son of Boardwalk pioneer Daniel B. Trimper, Granville was carrying on a family tradition of hospitality that dates back to the 1800s. Granville's wife, Pearl, ran the day-to-day operations of the property, which included the hotel and guest relations, the Coffee Shop and the Bar. Originally named "Inlet Casino" and later renamed "Inlet Hotel" in the early 1960s, the establishment was known for offering clean and affordable rooms to rent, a coffee shop with the best breakfast on the Boardwalk, a full-service bar and entertainment with live orchestras and dancing on the weekends. One of the more popular performers at the Inlet Casino in the late 1950s was Hank Clausen and his Hillbilly Orchestra.

Originally, the building was constructed without a bottom level and only half of the top third floor. Eventually, the Trimper family reimagined the building's potential and expanded it into a full three-story fixture with a total

The Inlet Lodge as it appeared in the 1950s in the otherwise barren downtown area. *Trimper's Rides Archive.*

The ocean view balcony of Trimper's Inlet Lodge overlooks passersby on the boardwalk as the Bar and Coffee Shop below are in full swing. *Trimper's Rides Archive.*

Inside the Inlet Lodge, near the stage where live bands would entertain guests in the mid-twentieth century, July 2019. *B.L. Strang-Moya.*

of thirty-four rooms and a double-decker porch offering unmatched views of bay sunsets and neighboring Assateague Island.

Anyone who steps inside the Coffee Shop, located on the Boardwalk level, will be transported back in time, with an exceedingly retro atmosphere that contrasts the modern, twenty-first-century Boardwalk just outside its walls. The original counter, stools, signage and fixtures, not to mention exceptional home cooking, provide an authentic and unparalleled experience for those who enjoy the simpler times of yesteryear.

Thirsty Boardwalk-goers can enjoy a cold pint opposite the Coffee Shop at the Bar, established in the Lodge around 1950 as the first bar on the Boardwalk and the second-oldest bar in Ocean City. Recently renovated, the establishment has a classic appeal with a jukebox, a vintage cigarette machine and a regularly rotating beer selection that prioritizes local breweries. Interestingly, the Bar once had a dumbwaiter, but it was covered up many years ago.

Locals and tourists measuring in the hundreds of thousands have enjoyed adult beverages at the Bar for nearly seventy years, but a particularly notable patron was none other than Bill Tracy. Tracy was on site for two weeks overseeing the installation and progress of the dark ride. It's said that he would end each day at the Bar (just a few doors down from the Haunted House) for dinner and drinks and then head off to bed in one of the Inlet Lodge rooms—a convenient home during his visit.

At times, members close to the Trimper family would enjoy the Lodge's conveniences too. Bob Cox, a longtime Trimper's Rides employee, lived in the basement of the Lodge year-round for many years. During the cold, harsh seaside winters, Cox would be the sole person in the building, ensuring that it was well kept. In fact, a special water heater was installed just for him. Cox was a critical figure in the Lodge's general upkeep and daily operations in the Coffee Shop and bar, as well as a major contributor to odd jobs around the amusement park. He passed away in 2016 after forty-five years of service to the Trimper family.

While the front bar can seat upward of twenty-five people, a few steps toward the back is the nostalgic open seating area complete with knotty pine walls, booths and various arcade games. It's in this section that the original entertainment and dancing of the twentieth century once occurred.

While the basement of the lodge has a few rooms, it's mostly used for storage, offices and workshops. Back in the day, what's now the storage room in the basement was a small gift shop that included a separate area offering bait and tackle equipment for the town's fishermen. Old nets and fishing rods are still tucked away from those days.

A simple, nostalgic neon sign points the way to the first bar in business on the Boardwalk. As of 2019, it remains the second-oldest bar in Ocean City. *Brandon Seidl.*

As for those who might feel spooked while inside the building—a tap on the shoulder, for instance, or a faint whisper in the year when no one is around—it's for good reason.

Trimper's Inlet Lodge is reportedly haunted and overrun by spirits from Ocean City's past. Some of these spirits are said to be Trimper family members. Countless stories of strange happenings in the lodge have been documented, and most of them can't be debunked by any simple explanation.

One year during the dead of winter, Brenda Parker, manager of the building at the time, was working in a room on the third level when she heard a door shut in the hallway. She was the only person in the building, but when she ventured into the hallway to investigate, she was surprised to find every one of the rooms' doors wide open.

On another night, the same manager, while serving a couple at the Bar, was interrupted by the patron she was attending to. The customer told her there was a man of medium build wearing a black fedora standing at the end of the Bar near the jukebox, quietly watching them. The man seemed as if he was going to choose a song to play, and when the customer approached him to inquire about his favorite songs, he vanished.

It was late at night, and the manager and couple were the only people in the establishment. Local lore states that Granville C. Trimper, father of the late Granville D. Trimper, suffered a heart attack behind the bar in 1953 and later died. Perhaps his spirit still roams the building, watching over his family's enterprise.

Multiple other occurrences have taken place through the years, cited by servers and cooks of the Coffee Shop. Hearing footsteps early in the morning and unknown noises are the most common. If you ever stop for a drink or a bite, keep an open mind. You just may come face-to-face with a character from the Boardwalk's past.

In 2011, the lodge's famous front oceanfront balcony was removed to address safety concerns, but the building's integrity and mystique otherwise remains the same. It's always ready for new guests of any age. Stop in for a meal, a beer, a place to stay or a paranormal experience. All are welcome—spirits and human beings alike.

5

Marty's Playland

Drop a coin in the slot. Test your skills. Collect your prize. It's a mesmerizing activity that beachgoers look forward to every summer, and it's rare to find a more satisfying place to try your luck than the resort's largest retro arcade venue, Marty's Playland, located on Worcester Street and the Boardwalk.

Marty's Playland arcade has been entertaining guests on Ocean City's famous Boardwalk since it opened in the early 1940s. It was one of the town's first complete arcade venues and has evolved to be a true amusement icon in the resort town that has not lost touch with its roots. Playland often finds itself on top-ten lists that recognize it as one of the most vintage and nostalgic arcades in the country. It acts as a time machine and allows visitors young and old to venture way back and experience a simpler time.

Playland was founded by Marty and Anna Mitnick. Mr. Mitnick was a veteran in the amusement industry and a successful operator of several coin machine arcades along the coast, including the Fountain Arcade in Philadelphia, Pennsylvania, which was a unique combination of a state-of-the-art arcade venue and a soda fountain. Mitnick was head of Associated Amusements for a time while working out of his showroom and service headquarters in Philadelphia in the mid-1940s.

The operation was later owned and managed by the Mitnicks' son-in-law, Sam Gaffin, until his retirement when he sold the enterprise to the Trimper family in 1991. Despite being one of the largest business transactions in Ocean City history at the time, the Trimper family swore to keep the arcade

Left: Marty's Playland as it looked in 1967. *Courtesy of Earl Shores.*

Below: Eventually, apartments were built above the arcade. The Playland Apartments remain some of the most affordable and comfortable accommodations on the boardwalk. *Trimper's Rides Archive.*

true to the spirit of yesteryear and not make any drastic changes, and they've since kept their vow.

Inside the dark, cavernous building filled with flashing lights and piercing sounds from every direction, a vast, impressive collection of video games, photobooths, '70s-era Skee-Ball lanes, Crane Diggers and pinball and redemption machines blend cutting-edge attractions with nostalgia and make a trip to the establishment truly stimulating. With prizes covering every square inch of wall space and a massive redemption counter, Playland offers the biggest prize selection and greatest variety of merchandise in town.

Vintage Crane Digger machines in the Diggerville area of Playland. *Brandon Seidl.*

Back in the good old days, players could turn in their hard-earned tickets for anything from trinkets like wax lips to cigarettes and lighters. Today, toys and technology-related prizes reign king. As of 2019, the arcade housed more than two hundred games and gives out approximately thirty-six million tickets each year to those who "play to win."

In conjunction with the full arcade operating on the first floor, Playland also offers several fully furnished vacation apartments on the second floor. The Playland Apartments, added as a second story to the original building, are an attractive vacation spot because of their waterfront views and convenience to the downtown area. Altogether, the arcade and the apartments above it account for more than twenty-four thousand square feet.

Back in the 1930s, the building acted as more of an amusement pavilion. Various attractions, including a miniature golf course and the ample coin-operated rides on the Boardwalk front, resided on what is now the back parking lot for the upstairs apartments. It was truly a catchall for those seeking entertainment, and it still is.

One of the time-honored and perhaps most classic attractions housed in the arcade is the Princess Doraldina Fortune Teller machine, which was

This page: Playland's Princess Doraldina Fortune Teller machine as she looks in 2019. *B.L. Strang-Moya.*

manufactured in 1928 by the Doraldina Corporation in Rochester, New York. It originally cost five cents to make the princess come to life. Her chest starts moving as if she's breathing, her arm sways over her tarot cards and the player's fortune is delivered and dispensed below.

Despite several makeovers during her nine-decade life span to repair her body parts, originally made of wax, and to touch up her cosmetics, Playland's princess remains as beautiful as ever and ready to vend your next lucky fortune. The fortune teller has been a showpiece at Marty's Playland since the arcade opened, but her location in the 1930s remains a mystery. Today, only a handful of the original machines exist nationwide, making Playland's prized "Gypsy," as many call her, all the more treasured by fans near and far.

March 30, 2008, marks the date of a nine-alarm fire that spread down Ocean City's famous Boardwalk. It destroyed the Dough Roller restaurant and severely damaged the Marty's Playland arcade and apartments in its wake. Recalling the Great Boardwalk Fire of 1925, help from neighboring towns was quickly summoned at the start of the blaze and included more than 225 firefighters from nineteen neighboring towns.

As a result of the fire, two Skee-Ball games were burned and all of them suffered water damage. Ten other classic arcade games, including Crane Diggers and Bowlingos, were lost in the blaze. Four Playland apartments were severely damaged but saved by the firemen and the sprinkler system. Three apartments were completely lost, as well as the arcade's original hardwood floors.

Playland's famous Skee-Ball lanes date back to the 1970s. *Brandon Seidl.*

Overhauled Playland sign and front as it appeared in 2007. *Courtesy of H. Michael Heath.*

On July 15, 2008, the arcade, including the classic Skee-Ball machines and vintage Crane Diggers, was back open for business. The new Dough Roller restaurant, rebuilt next door on the same site, opened prior to the 2009 season. On August 1, 2008, the cause of the fire was declared arson, and the suspect was arrested.

Marty's Playland was most recently managed by the late Christopher Trimper until the fall of 2019. Today, the arcade and apartments are operated by fourth- and fifth-generation members of the Trimper family and their dedicated employees.

6

The Plim Plaza Cupola and Other Historic Hotels

Visitors stand and stare at the cupola from the Boardwalk below, but a full explanation of that piece, and all other unique adornments of the Boardwalk's many historic hotels, requires a quick journey through the past.

For centuries, the peninsula known today as Ocean City was home only to Algonquin tribes whose livelihood and culture stemmed from seaside and forest resources lining the coasts of Maryland and Virginia.

That might be a little too far back. But in the seventeenth century, the Maryland piece of the peninsula, along with a slice of coastal Delaware to the north, was acquired by Englishman Thomas Fenwick through a land grant from Lord Baltimore. At that point, Ocean City could be reached only by stagecoach and ferry, though it still served as a popular summer destination for residents of Worcester County's mainland.

In 1867, the town was dubbed the "Ladies' Resort to the Ocean" by one of its early landowners, Stephen Tabor. In 1869, businessman Isaac Coffin opened the first beachside hotel and tavern, the Rhode Island Inn, later known as Ocean House, to accommodate paying guests. In 1875, while a railroad to the beach was under construction, the Atlantic Hotel Company christened the town "Ocean City" and opened the resort's first major hotel, the Atlantic Hotel, complete with four hundred rooms and billiards. The hotel has been owned by the Purnell family since 1923.

Tourists began to travel to the shore via the new railway by 1878, and more and more hotels popped up along the beach during the latter half of the nineteenth century. Congress Hall Hotel, the Seaside Hotel, Windsor

Resort and the Plimhimmon Hotel were among a handful of summertime lodges to open their doors before the century turned.

Sadly, none of their original structures remains standing today. Congress Hall was eventually purchased by the Trimper family, and the site of the hotel became part of the amusement complex. Windsor Resort simply became Trimper's Rides. The Seaside and the Atlantic Hotels both met tragic ends in the infamous fire of 1925, but only the Atlantic was rebuilt.

Much of Ocean City's history has been shaped by fires. One of Ocean City's many early hotels, the Plimhimmon, built in 1894, also surrendered to a major fire in 1962. During an expansion of the hotel, flames broke out in the building's north wing after the mishandling of electrical equipment, and the blaze spread through the wooden structure. At the time, it was one of the biggest fires ever fought by the Ocean City Volunteer Fire Company. More than four hundred firefighters from fourteen nearby fire companies joined forces to quell the flames.

Only parts of the hotel's south wing avoided any damage, and part of that wing still remains standing today. In 2012, when carpenters at the Plimhimmon—by then known as the Plim Plaza Hotel—were replacing siding on the poolside of the hotel, they found burnt timbers and old-fashioned peg joinery.

Contrary to popular belief, the hotel's famous bell-shaped cupola isn't an original piece of the building's structure that was uncovered from the ash. In 1963, the hotel was rebuilt, and a fifth floor, along with a new cupola modeled after the older one that was lost to the flames, was added. In 1970, the Harrison family purchased the Plimhimmon and changed the name to Plim Plaza.

The cupola atop the Plim Plaza Hotel as it appeared in 1985. The original cupola was lost to a fire in 1962, and the current bell-shaped dome was modeled on the old one when the hotel was rebuilt in 1963. *John Margolies/Library of Congress.*

But even if the tall, gray dome isn't an Ocean City artifact from the town's first hotel boom, its presence, royally sitting atop the hotel right on Second Street at the Boardwalk, is a nostalgia-tinged reminder of Ocean City's early years. While the hotel's interior and exterior were updated and modernized in its 1960s revival, the newer cupola is nearly identical to the original. Squint your eyes a little, look up and just imagine you're standing at the heart of the Lady's Resort to the Ocean about 1894.

Aside from the Plim Plaza and its elegantly old-fashioned cupola, there are myriad other tributes to Ocean City days of old that can be spotted along the Boardwalk—many of them hotels pushing a century of life.

On Eighth Street, the Lankford Hotel has weathered its share of storms since 1924 and is said to be the best preserved of all the old hotels in Ocean City. The property, which is made up of the main hotel, the nine-apartment Ayresbuilt, the three-floor Sea Robin, the Lankford Lodge and six commercial storefront properties on and below the Boardwalk, has remained in the same family for its near-century lifetime and has passed through four generations of female owners.

Though it was demolished in 1990, the stately Washington Hotel on Tenth Street stood eighty feet high with eight stories and was the tallest building in Ocean City from 1931, when it was built, to 1970. It was also the largest wooden building in Maryland. It came down in 1990 in part because of fire code violations. The George Washington had slot machines until they were made illegal. The hotel was also rumored to have been a hotbed for illegal liquor during Prohibition and to have been partially funded by illegal liquor sales.

A year before the George Washington was built, the Commander Hotel on the Boardwalk at Fourteenth Street opened on Memorial Day in 1930. The original building was expanded in 1948 and completely razed in 1997. The current building opened in the spring of 1998. When it was built, the original Commander stood alone as Ocean City's most northern hotel. It notably boasted Ocean City's first elevator, its first in-room telephone service and a sweeping front porch that overlooked the beach and north end of the Boardwalk, which was extended past the Commander to Twenty-Sixth Street in 1950. During its early years, a week's stay at the hotel, including three square meals a day, cost ninety-five dollars.

When visitors sought haven at the Commander during World War II, the windows would be covered at night by blackout curtains due to the danger of enemy shelling by off-shore submarines. A decade or so after the war, families would travel from all over Maryland and beyond to attend a Commander Clambake complete with lobster, corn on the cob and steamed clams.

These are just a few shining examples of hotels that were originally built in the early twentieth century and have lasted well into the twenty-first. Mid-century modern motels have also endured, though most of them are located just past the Boardwalk in what's considered the start of Ocean City's midtown area. However, the Santa Maria, one of the first motels to make up Motel Row, is located on the Boardwalk at Fifteenth Street. When it was built in 1956, it boasted a swimming pool and a television in every room. Of course, even as late as 1966, Ocean City's cable television system offered only five channels.

While they're few and far between, even older beach cottages can be found dotting the Boardwalk's northern half. The Inn on the Ocean, for example, was built in 1932 by then mayor of Ocean City William McCabe and his wife, Harriet. It's still run as a charming bed-and-breakfast with pristine views of the beach and Boardwalk at Tenth Street.

7

𝒯𝑜𝑛𝑦'𝑠 𝒫𝑖𝑧𝑧𝑎 𝒞𝒽𝑒𝑓

The Plim's cupola isn't the only architectural landmark that gets onlookers looking up in wonder. Tony's Pizza Chef, another rooftop oddity, has been serving the same statuesque pizza pie for more than four decades.

Located on Atlantic Avenue on the Boardwalk, Tony's Pizza is an Italian restaurant that has nourished hungry beachgoers since 1972. The mustachioed Pizza Chef stands eleven feet tall on Tony's rooftop deck and wears a white chef's coat; red, green and white striped pants; and a chef's hat that reads "Tony's Pizza." He also holds a pizza, complete with toppings that look like they could be pepperoni, onion and green peppers, bordered by little lightbulbs around the crust that illuminate the statue in the night.

Another pizza chef just like the one atop Tony's lives at Vince's Pizza in Rochelle, Illinois. That one was purchased in 1971 by a traveling salesman in a Wienermobile, while the Tony's statue was purchased several years later at a restaurant show. The two chefs look almost identical at first glance, but the trim on the Vince's statue's clothing is slightly different. He

The look of Tony's Pizza Chef has been altered slightly over the years. Here, in 1985, the chef donned plaid pants and a red-buttoned jacket, while today his outfit is red, white and green and striped rather than plaid. *John Margolies/Library of Congress.*

also has bulbs on the button of his jacket rather than on the pizza, and his hat, of course, reads "Vince's" instead of "Tony's Pizza." There was another similar statue at the Goody Goody Diner in St. Louis, Missouri, from 1975 to 1988, and other pizza chefs with different heads (the Vince's and Tony's model was altered because Vince's owner apparently thought the original head looked more Mexican than Italian) can be found in North Carolina, Michigan, Minnesota and Tennessee.

8
Art Sale, Baby!

O ne of Ocean City's most iconic oddities celebrated its fiftieth birthday in the summer of 2017. Eccentric, extravagant and just a little bit loud—how one might describe Ocean City in the summertime—is, not coincidentally, how one would most definitely describe Ocean Gallery at all times of the year.

"Art sale, baby!" is the motto exclaimed by the gallery's proprietor and founder, Joe Kroart. "It's astounding!" is another slogan of his, but in almost

Ocean Gallery lights up a summer night in 2018. *B.L. Strang-Moya.*

all of the homemade and purposely kitschy commercials in which Kroart stars, he's repeating "Art sale, baby!" over and over and over again. In one commercial, he rides a bicycle off the gallery roof. Bystanders scream as a dummy hits the boardwalk, but then it's Joe again in his standard black tux and red bowtie getup, standing up unharmed and waving his arms frantically in the next scene.

Ocean Gallery has a long and understandably outlandish history after more than fifty years in Ocean City. Inside the gallery there's a lot to unpack—figuratively and, with probably more art per square inch than anywhere else in the world, literally as well.

You can almost smell the oil paint fumes when you approach Ocean Gallery from Second Street, where its street- and parking lot–facing exterior walls are as bright and outlandish as its storefront on the Boardwalk. Behind the building, Day-Glo Homer and Bart Simpson cutouts wait for passersby to stick their face in the holes and pose for photos, while art cars—usually a Batmobile, and a *Titanic* before it met its fate at the bottom of the ocean—provide additional quirky photo ops. And the Art Cars are only the start.

ART CARS

The Batmobile began its long and exciting career as a humble 1968 Dodge Charger. It provided transportation for Joe Kroart's sons to and from school, although they thought it was old and ugly and were embarrassed by it, so they'd get dropped off two blocks away, where no one would see them get out. It would later become, arguably, the most famous vehicle in Maryland.

In 1989, during the height of the Batman movie craze, Kroart's son Joey suggested they turn their old Dodge into a Batmobile of their very own. Kroart was never one to shoot down a crazy idea, and they'd been selling Batman movie posters out of the Boardwalk gallery by the dozen. Sensing a fun art project that might also serve as a clever marketing gimmick, the father-and-son team transformed the car overnight.

They used body filler, cans of spray paint and recycled parts, all costing about thirty dollars in total, and turned the old clunker into Batman's preferred mode of transport—or at least something that slightly resembled it. It was its own special version of the Batmobile, complete with adornments like rubber bats, little American flags, a hairdryer, a metal fan (and an adjoining cardboard sign, "Batman has many fans!"), scrap metal and a

When not on the street on display, the Batmobile resides in the garage under Ocean Gallery. *B.L. Strang-Moya.*

German candelabra, which was a wedding gift from one of the Kroart's friends, who was disappointed by seeing the gift stuck to the hood of a car.

Alongside all the miscellany today is a cardboard sign that reads, "Please Touch." Kroart cited the sign as a way to make people feel comfortable around artistic expressions; he often overhears parents telling their kids not to touch the decorated car, to which the kids often reply, "But it says I can!"

Laura Kroart, the youngest of Kroart's three children, remembered being in first grade when a classmate pulled out a framed photo of him and his brother standing proudly in front of the Batmobile for show and tell.

"That's my dad's car," Laura exclaimed.

"No, it's not," replied the classmate. "It's the Batmobile."

Throughout the years it has spent on the road and parked on the side of its home at the Boardwalk Art Gallery, the Batmobile has brought immeasurable joy to onlookers of every age. On occasion, it's been lent to charity fundraisers to benefit underprivileged and disabled children. Kroart recalled toll booth attendants at the Bay Bridge being thrilled to see the vehicle drive through, and there have been times when even state troopers had to stifle their laughter while seeing the handcrafted superhero car driving down the road.

"There are so many things in life that are serious and really tough for people to bear," Kroart once said. "I think making people smile and laugh and making them happy is a very important thing, and that's what the Batmobile does."

Now more than fifty years old, the car sometimes hibernates in its Bat Cave, the garage underneath the gallery. It's not driven around town as much as it was decades earlier. But when its unbelievably loud engine is revved and the car is paraded down Coastal Highway, which does happen on occasion, it can be unclear just who's behind the steering wheel. It could be Kroart, but it could also be the very superhero of Gotham City.

"Batman retired 20 years ago and possibly came to Ocean City, shunned publicity and quietly opened an art gallery," Kroart once explained to reporter Susan Canfora of the *Daily Times*. "The reason he came out of retirement is to fight crime. But there isn't a lot of crime here in Ocean City, so he's taking it easy. And that's why he has time to drive the Batmobile around on Coastal Highway."

While the Batmobile is the most famous of Kroart's art cars, there are more—many more. They're made not for money, of which they make absolutely none, but for the pure joy of creating a mobile work of art almost always out of recycled parts and materials.

Another memorable mobile creation of Kroart's is the *Titanic* car, which was sunk to the bottom of the Atlantic Ocean in August 2001, to become part of Ocean City's artificial reef. That one was an old Cadillac that was reworked into the *Titanic* after about two and a half hours of work in Kroart's driveway.

A small lifeboat on the trunk, a propeller on the back bumper, an antenna for the radio ("for distress calls only"), life preservers, the ship's

log (a literal log with "TITANIC" scrawled across it) and handmade smokestacks were all part of the décor. On August 26, 2001, it was filled with dry ice, and steam came out of the windows as it sank into the ocean—an Ocean City oddity that lives at the bottom of the sea.

An artistic, digitally altered depiction of the *Titanic* car, which was propelled into the Atlantic Ocean in 2001 to become part of Ocean City's artificial reef. *Courtesy of Joe Kroart.*

There's also the old Buick that's spending its second life as the "Cow Car." Kroart and his sons drove it to Laura's nursery school one day to surprise her. They parked far away from the building so as not to disturb the students, but apparently, they hadn't parked far enough away.

"We get out of the Cow Car, and we start walking towards the building—all the kids' faces are plastered against the window with their eyes as big as saucers," Kroart recalled. "Everybody in the whole school was looking at the Cow Car!"

The Cow Car's still kicking, they say, and one day they might even breed it.

But if there's an Art Car in Ocean City that's seen by more people than any other, the Batmobile might have a little competition with the Ocean Gallery Immobile Unit—the truck on the roof of the gallery, which, unlike the other cars, doesn't spend any time in a garage. It can't because it was literally nailed to the roof.

Kroart was inspired by a bar in California that had a Cadillac sticking out of its roof. He'd been doing a weather report for WBAL-TV in Baltimore, broadcasting the forecast in Ocean City from outside the gallery. He nailed the truck to the roof for atmosphere, he said, adding to the potpourri of other odd objects attached to the building's exterior, but he also used it to report the weather. He christened it the WLIF Ocean Gallery Immobile Unit.

OCEAN GALLERY—IT'S ASTOUNDING!

The art cars are secondary to their headquarters, which is a three-story art gallery on the Ocean City Boardwalk that's a shining beacon of light on a busy summer night. Among other things, it features neon splashes of color and art and signs and a hodgepodge of items—string lights, flags and cement pawprints, supposedly from Susan Sarandon's dog—nailed to its outside walls, while Christmas music plays outside nearly all year.

In 2017, the mayor and the Maryland comptroller honored Ocean Gallery owner Joe Kroart for fifty years in Ocean City. Although the gallery's current structure isn't quite that old (though it has been around for decades), Ocean Gallery's earliest iteration did first come to Ocean City in 1967.

Kroart came to Ocean City on a summer break during college. The trunk of his car was loaded with his own paintings, and he had the simple goal of spending five or six weeks in town surviving off the sales of his artwork alone.

His first "store" was the rented storefront of a chicken carryout restaurant, where he paid the owner 20 percent of his sales and slept in a storeroom underneath the building. "Because he didn't have much money, a fly-infested basement was all that he could afford," explains Joey Kroart on the Ocean Gallery website. "During especially tough weeks, Kroart was known to actually eat the flys [*sic*], concocting a variety of different recipes for fly cuisine. More on that some other time."

He spent the entirety of his days that summer painting on the beach and working the occasional odd job. One customer owned a piano and organ store in Baltimore, for example, and asked Kroart to paint some publicity shots.

"He said, 'I want you to paint my wife's stomach when she's in a bikini with her girlfriend, and I want "Bernie Shofer's" on one stomach and "Piano and Organs" on the other,'" Kroart explained. "So, I said, 'okay.' They came in two-piece bathing suits, they laid on the beach mat and I began to paint their stomachs with that lettering. And they were both really ticklish. And he stood there with his cigar for about forty-five minutes, and we got this painting done, and he was very pleased. They walked the beach all day advertising his piano and organ company."

The space he was allotted to sell his paintings was very narrow and very high, which gave him plenty of wall space. Kroart said that the high ceilings made it look more impressive than it really was.

"I also found that even when things are partially covered, people still identify with something they like, so I got triple the display space with the overlap," he said. "The more I overlap, I realized it was more inviting.... [It's] almost overwhelming, but it's very challenging to people and it's very interesting and fascinating."

The idea of overlapping artwork would be amplified tenfold a few years later when Kroart moved the gallery into its permanent home, which he says holds the record for the most artwork per square inch of anywhere in the world.

That first year, Kroart was broke by Labor Day, but he considers the endeavor a success because he was able to survive off the sale of his art, thanks, in part, to fly cuisine and Bernie Shofer. The next summer, his business moved to the porch of the Colonial Hotel on First Street, where he had to move his inventory outside every day and back inside every night. When the hotel burned down in 1970, Kroart was forced to move the gallery once again. The next location would be on the Boardwalk at Second Street, and it's where Ocean Gallery would remain. What had previously been a hotel called the Beach Way was transformed into a beachside art gallery.

"If you walk around in the building, you'll see the hallways are the same—our framing counter was one apartment, sometimes you can see a

This early location of Ocean Gallery is a bit more modest than its current home on Second Street and the Boardwalk. *Courtesy of Joe Kroart.*

little bit of tile behind paintings where a bathroom was," Laura said. "He kind of just came through with a sledgehammer and made it all one place."

The building, under all of its layers of paint and lights and signage, was architecturally inspired by fifteenth-century Dutch churches, but the items he started adding to the gallery once its structure was in place mostly came from Baltimore. It took seventeen years to build, but it may never really be complete.

In 1972, Kroart installed a bay window that he'd salvaged and used it to showcase artwork. People started paying attention, so he took the idea one step further. Stained glass, siding, a coal chute—those were items he'd salvaged from demolished rowhomes and had been storing in his farmhouse. He simply attached them to the gallery's exterior walls for the spectacle.

These items were painted bright yellow, red, blue and white. Christmas lights and silver reflectors were tacked on too. Kroart said that everyone was telling him to paint the Ocean Gallery sign—that is, the one that actually spells "OCEAN GALLERY" in huge letters on the roof—in gold to make it look expensive. He opted for fluorescent red instead and ran lights around it in case it didn't already stand out enough.

Kroart's showmanship exemplifies just one quality, of surprisingly many, that he shares with legendary circus industry professional P.T. Barnum. Both believe in "getting people under the tent," luring them in with the spectacle, and then awing them with all the wonders inside. Kroart is also quick to add that he and Barnum shared the same stature, six foot three and 210 pounds; both had three children; and both lived on an eighteen-acre farm—when Kroart's not working in Ocean City, he's at his farmhouse in Monkton. Kroart's three-ring circus just happens to be a three-floor gallery.

Said Kroart to John Woestendiek of the *Baltimore Sun*, "I don't push anything down anybody's throat. I just put it out, like a buffet."

The outside of the building is a work of art, but what's inside its walls can't be forgotten either. Kroart says there are thirty to forty thousand pieces of art in the gallery at any given moment. The works range from dorm room posters and condo-friendly beach scenes to abstract paintings and watercolor and oil depictions of Maryland landscapes.

It's one of only a handful of galleries that is licensed to sell original works by Leroy Neiman. You can also find photographs by A. Aubrey Bodine, paintings of Ocean City by Paul McGehee and signed prints by David Schroeder, an artist who works in the framing department. There are some items in the gallery that cost ninety-nine cents and some that go up to a couple thousand dollars, though most pieces aren't more than a few hundred dollars.

Kroart believes in presenting fine art as entertainment—it's more accessible that way.

"I don't like to use the word 'art' in anything we do," he said. "We're an attraction. Because when you say 'art,' it turns people off. They get scared; they're intimidated; they feel they don't know enough about it to talk about it. But we're just the opposite. Everything here is wild and crazy but not in any way negative—you gotta be careful with the crazy stuff. You walk a fine line."

Shocking people without offending anyone is a very fine line to walk, he noted.

Ocean Gallery founder Joe Kroart works behind the gallery's front counter in the summer of 2018. *B.L. Strang-Moya.*

It is said that Kroart never met a gimmick he didn't like, and this may be true. In almost every press photo, he's "screaming," or standing with his arms waving over his head and his mouth wide open ("I found a way to communicate through a photograph," he said), and scattered throughout the gallery are photos of Kroart, always in a tuxedo (the same one for decades, which he bought used from a Towson rental store), linking arms and shaking hands with celebrities. Some of them are of the boardwalk Jack Sparrow and Marilyn Monroe variety, but some of them are actual models, actresses and politicians.

But a cardboard sign on the stairs reminds visitors, "The most important person to ever visit Ocean Gallery is…You!"

Kroart recalled a time when his good friend and her mother were sitting on a bench outside the gallery—one just across the boardwalk that faced the gallery's entrance. As people were walking in and out of the store, Kroart got up on the counter—visible through the open-garage-door front entrance—and started dancing. His friend went into hysterics, and her mother couldn't understand what she was laughing at. He quickly jumped down before the mother saw and started waiting on customers again. She was trying to explain what had happened to her mother, while still doubled over in laughter.

When asked about his fondest memory from all his years at Ocean Gallery, Kroart simply responds, "The people….There are thousands of stories like this—people coming in and we make a connection that's so personal," he said. "It's humbling to know this, but it's so personal that they come back years later and tell us about something they got that made a difference in their lives or an experience they've never forgotten."

Stumble upon the gallery in the summertime, and you might even encounter an Artist of the Day—children of six or seven years old who paint at a desk at the front of the store, price their artwork and sell it to customers. The money they make goes straight into their college funds.

Gallery employees remembered one little artist whose parents couldn't get her to leave the gallery at the end of the day because she was having too much fun.

It's not unusual for someone to enter Ocean Gallery, get lost in the maze of photographs and paintings and prints and posters and decide they never want to leave the place. Past the dogs playing poker and tributes to mid-century Hollywood stars, art connoisseurs find stunning pieces by artists of local and national acclaim and discover masterpieces by artists whose names they'd never heard before. And people who never would have thought to step foot in an art gallery realize that art is not so scary after all.

Pip the Beach Cat

One of Ocean Gallery's biggest fans is orange, four-legged and furry. Pip the Beach Cat hangs out in the gallery all the time, usually near a wooden sign at the front of the store that says, "OCEAN GALLERY LOVES 'PIP!'" because Ocean Gallery is as big a fan of Pip as Pip is of the gallery.

Pip became locally famous after his owner, Emily Meadows, posted a video of him riding a boogie board on the shallow part of the shoreline, where the surf meets the sand. Pip is about as fearless and mischievous as he is tiny and cute. When Meadows posted more photos of him digging holes in the sand, playing on the boardwalk, posing with Fisher's Popcorn, Dumser's ice cream and orange crushes and generally gallivanting about town, he quickly amassed a cult following on social media and even started "writing" a book, though it's rumored that Meadows is his ghostwriter.

From the ocean to Ocean Gallery, Pip's pictures and videos serve as a guide for his followers, many of whom are kids, to show them all the cool things to do in Ocean City.

Pip the Beach Cat is a regular at Ocean Gallery. *Courtesy of Emily Meadows.*

"People are connecting with him because there's been a need to show Ocean City in this sort of way," Meadows said, "but also because he's showing everyone another side of cats. You don't need to just sit in the window and lay in the sun all day, you can go out and do stuff."

Almost an Oddity: Boathenge

If the gallery and the cars weren't enough, Ocean City would have had its own nautical version of Stonehenge if it were up to Kroart.

"Boathenge" was conceived by Kroart's son Joey in January 2007 as a technique the town could use to market itself and draw in more tourists, particularly those attracted to roadside (in this case, beachside) anomalies. Boathenge would consist of old, out-of-commission boats faced bow down in astronomical alignment—a megalithic semicircle in the sand à la Stonehenge or its modern-day midwestern cousin, Carhenge.

Kroart stuck a sign in the sand that said, "Proposed Site of Boathenge." He put a call out for retired, hole-ridden boats and soon collected twenty-six of them through donations.

Unfortunately, Boathenge was not written in the stars for Ocean City. While four out of seven city council members voted to push the project forward, the proposal was nixed by the department of natural resources in fall 2008, due to a restriction on creating a permanent structure on the beach because of the hazard its debris could create during a major storm.

"Stonehenge wasn't built in a day," Kroart said.

9
Randy Hofman's Sand Sculptures

Not all art is intended to be permanent. The pieces that line the walls of Ocean Gallery can be purchased, hung and enjoyed for a lifetime. Randy Hofman's art in the sand, though, lasts only as long as the natural elements allow.

A walk on the boards isn't complete without a look at the biblical sand sculptures that Hofman creates on the beach, which face the Boardwalk on Second Street between Plim Plaza and Ocean Gallery year-round. All of the intricate details of Hofman's temporary Renaissance art are best seen by the light of the sun, and at night, colored lights that illuminate the sculptures provide an alternate view against the backdrop of the dark sky. Both are different but equally beautiful views and should be enjoyed by daylight and in the dark to truly get the full effect.

Hofman knew he wanted to be an artist as early as second grade. He began his artistic journey as an oil painter and studied advertising design and visual communications at Pratt Institute before coming to Ocean City in 1974. Hofman eventually ended up studying sand sculpting under Marc Altamar, the artist who started the sand series in Ocean City in the early 1970s. When Altamar moved to Florida in 1981, Hofman took the reins and carried on the tradition, creating one of the most-photographed landmarks on the Boardwalk time and time again.

Hofman's sculpting tools of choice include his hands and a plastic crab knife for the smaller details. A mixture of water and glue keep the sculptures in place and can keep them preserved for up to several weeks at

One of Hofman's sculptures is illuminated in the night. *Courtesy of Gerald Uhlan.*

Over the years, Hofman has created custom sand sculptures for couples who marry on Ocean City's beach. *Brandon Seidl.*

Evangelical artist Randy Hofman uses a shovel to carve a sand sculpture depicting the face of Jesus. *Brandon Seidl.*

a time. Volunteers with the Son'Spot Ministry will often dig up the mounds of sand for Hofman to carve into. Hofman, an ordained minister, uses the visual medium to communicate the message of his ministry. On many occasions, he's been hired to create sand sculptures for couples about to be engaged or married.

He has often pointed out that his sculptures are as temporary as our lives on the physical plane. Because it's temporary, he says, it's more precious.

Notably, Hofman was one of many to be involved in Ocean City's attempt to build the world's largest sandcastle—at least by the Guinness Book of World Records' standards—in summer of 1990. The finished product was forty feet tall and missed the world record by only two inches. On the bright side, the town did receive a good amount of publicity from the attempt, and tourists were able to walk to the top of the sand structure for one dollar. Today, Hofman's sandcastles are much less extravagant but just as engaging and meaningful.

10

Landmark Characters of the Boardwalk

More than anything, it's the people who really make the Boardwalk what it is. The amusements and shops are almost secondary to what really permeates the imaginations of those who have walked the boards over the years—the characters. The friends people meet, the family they've made memories with and all the loveable weirdos they've encountered along the way are what most make the Boardwalk such a magical place. And "weirdo" is a term of endearment here, of course.

Aside from iconic and lovably weird businessmen like Joe Kroart and Bill Tracy, there is a long list of Boardwalk buskers who have captured the hearts of vacationers from every corner of the world.

Tony Button is one well-known busker of the twenty-first century, but he's better known as the Gold Man. His whole body is covered in a layer of gold, and he spends his summer days on the Boardwalk sitting on a three-wheeled bicycle and squeaking through a whistle in his mouth. (This is Button's full-time job; in the winter, he flies south to perform in Florida.) There is also Joseph Smith, better known by his pseudonym the Amazing Josini, who delights children with an act that's two parts magic, one part comedy and one part puppeteering, and William Campion, who wears a Mad Hatter–style top hat and crafts balloon animals from the seat of his motorized wheelchair.

The buskers, for the most part, are beloved by all, save a handful of city council members who have been attempting to place limits on where, when and how performers can make their livings on the Boardwalk since the mid-twentieth century. Most recently, in 2015, these limits were deemed unconstitutional and in violation of the performers' First Amendment rights to free speech. The aforementioned buskers, plus countless other artists, musicians and costumed entertainers, continue to perform on the Boardwalk all summer long. You can find them there until 1:00 a.m., which is one major provision that was allowed by the courts in the town's street performer ordinance.

Earlier performers, now relegated to the history books of Boardwalk entertainment, include blind musicians Tex and Shorty, who were always accompanied by ten-gallon hat and banjo, and Bozo the Clown, who sat in a dunk tank at the pier amusements and was notorious for hurling insults at passersby.

"He sat in a cage and you tried to dump him in the water by hitting a target with baseballs," remembered Ocean City lover JJ_Walters in an OceanCity.com forum thread dedicated to Ocean City nostalgia. "Nothing special about this, but it was Bozo himself who was, how shall I say it, 'unique.' This guy would taunt you with all kinds of derogatory insults! 'Your girlfriend is so ugly…' That kind of stuff. Not exactly family-friendly stuff, but for a teenager, it was hilarious! Bozo got the boot sometime around the late '80s, early '90s."

BOARDWALK ELVIS

The most iconic Boardwalk busker to ever make a name for himself in Ocean City is, without a doubt, the incomparable Boardwalk Elvis. Elvis, who also answered to his given name, Norman Webb, is the only street performer to have his own exhibit in the Ocean City Life-Saving Station Museum. He's also the only one to have received a key to the city from the Ocean City mayor and city council, which was bestowed on Webb in May 2018, less than a month before he would pass away. Webb had been battling cancer and died on June 16, 2018, at the age of seventy-eight.

Webb's career on the Boardwalk started in the 1960s, when he began walking up and down the boards with a boombox on his shoulder. He dressed up as a number of characters, including a cowboy, a beatnik and a surfer, but it was in the 1970s when he added the famous white Elvis jumpsuit to his act (though not before he donned an absurdly bright lime green leisure suit). The crowd loved it, and the Elvis character stuck.

"All day, every day he would cruise up and down the boards in his polyester shirt and pants and [cowboy] hat, while carrying an old eight-track cassette

Above: A Boardwalk Elvis postcard circa mid-1990s. *Authors' collections.*

Right: Boardwalk Elvis poses with his boom box in August 1993, near the stage for the Ocean City Beach Boys concert. *David Seidl.*

recorder which always played Elvis tunes, while humming along with a kazoo," JJ_Walters wrote, recalling Webb's act from the 1980s.

In the '90s, when *Time* magazine ran a story that mentioned Ocean City and included a picture of Webb in full Elvis regalia, the town bought Webb a Greyhound ticket and a couple of nights' lodging in Graceland for him and a friend.

Later in his life, Webb was often spotted riding his bicycle from his home in Showell, Maryland, to Ocean City. In 2013, he was hit by a car while making the daily journey on his bike but was able to walk away with only a few minor injuries. His bike, on the other hand, was smashed to pieces. After hearing about the accident, a local radio show raised $678 in under an hour—a testament to how beloved Webb was by tourists and locals alike—and the show bought beloved Boardwalk Elvis a new electric bike with a backup battery, lights and a basket.

11

Boardwalk Trains

By Karl Schwarz

I n June 1963, Sam Mochella requested the city council's permission to operate a train on the Boardwalk, one that would be similar to the trains operating at several Florida resorts. After exploring several concerns, in July, the council granted permission for a two-week trial. The trial did not go well; the train was larger and heavier than expected, which damaged the Boardwalk and drew complaints from visitors. After the failed Boardwalk trial, the train was permitted to operate as a sightseeing tour along Baltimore Avenue as part of the bus franchise for the remainder of the 1963 season. In December, the council declined to renew permission for the train to operate in the 1964 season, as it was considering having the city operate its own boardwalk train service.

In March 1964, after reviewing similar amusement train operations in Wildwood, New Jersey, and Virginia Beach, Virginia, the city council decided to purchase two trains for $14,288 from National Amusement Company in Dayton, Ohio. The green trains began operating in early June 1964. Each train had a gasoline-powered engine that pulled five single-axle coaches and could carry thirty people. One-way fare to travel the length of the boardwalk was twenty-five cents.

This train was such a success that after only a few weeks of operation, the city council began exploring obtaining a third train, which arrived just in time for the 1965 season. A fourth Jeep-based unit built by Polytechnic Industries in Snow Hill, Maryland, was added in 1966 and operated until the end of the 1971 season. This train's design proved undependable, as its

A green Boardwalk train of the 1960s. *Courtesy of Karl Schwarz.*

enclosed Jeep- and later Ford-based drivetrain were not well suited for the train's slow stop-and-go operations.

In 1966, the staff members operating the trains were issued uniforms to foster a more consistent professional appearance, and the fare was increased to fifty cents. Around 1968, the four trains were repainted white. The early days of the train operation created controversy, as Ocean City's private city bus franchise operator (and cousin to Hugh T. Cropper Jr., the town's mayor at the time) filed a lawsuit with the Maryland Public Service Commission alleging that Ocean City was operating a competing "common carrier" without state approval. The town lost the suit but then took over bus operations in 1965 and resolved the issue.

The original fleet of trains served the city well, but by 1970, the original units needed replacement. Although its greater weight and wider body were concerns, the Chance Manufacturing Starliner train model was selected, as it offered better power and braking. The $50,000 cost of three new trains was spread over two seasons, with new coaches purchased for the 1970 season and new Star Lounge engines purchased for the 1971 season. Two more Starliner trains were added—one in 1972 and another in 1973. These trains had an engine and three coaches and could carry a total of about seventy-five passengers. Eventually, six of these trains were operating on the boardwalk. The Starliner engines were used on the boardwalk until the early 1990s.

In 1991, one engine was replaced with a modified Jeep Wrangler, and in 1992, two more engines were replaced. The Starliner passenger coaches were periodically replaced but remained in use and were pulled by these Jeeps through the 2002 season.

In 2003, eight completely new trains were purchased from Trams International for $1.5 million and put into operation. Each train has an engine and two thirty-eight-person coaches. On May 26, 2013, one of these train's engines was destroyed by a fire that ignited during refueling. A modified Jeep was used as a replacement engine to pull one train during the 2013–18 seasons. In August 2018, the city council authorized purchase of eight replacement trains at a total cost of $1.4 million. These trains were towed by modified Jeep Wranglers that each pulled two forty-passenger coaches. These trains began operating in the summer 2019 season and are supported by a new maintenance facility at Second Street. For the summer 2019 season, the fare for a one-way trip on the Boardwalk was raised to $4.

Since the trains started operating, the city has sought to ensure safe Boardwalk co-use between pedestrians and the train. The 1999 reconstruction of the southern end of the Boardwalk resolved several issues, as it provided a concrete lane east of the Boardwalk that runs from Third Street to the pier. The bottleneck west of the pier building, where the Boardwalk is only twenty-two feet wide, was also resolved in 1999 by rerouting the train to cross the pier east of the amusement area.

The train station at the north end of the Boardwalk was built in 1991 and is a replica of the original 1892 railroad station located on Baltimore Avenue at South Division Street. The train station at the south end of the Boardwalk was built in 2000, replacing a much less attractive station built in 1979.

In 2018, the trains carried more than 445,000 people along the boardwalk during the summer and more than 100,000 people through Northside Park during Ocean City's annual holiday light show, Winterfest of Lights.

12

Gone but Not Forgotten

THE OLD BANDSTAND

The old bandstand has been lost to time, but there's still a plaque commemorating the retired landmark right on Somerset Street and the Boardwalk, where the bandstand once jutted grandly off onto the beach.

The original Bandstand was an open-air porch on the Boardwalk erected by Frank Townsend, who served as the town doctor in the early twentieth century and also purchased various properties downtown and on the Boardwalk. He had the structure built across from his pharmacy on Somerset Street. Concerts in the bandstand were led by Frank Sacca, a local hotelier and accomplished musician, and shows by the Ocean

A vintage Ocean City postcard features the Boardwalk bandstand in the early 1950s. *Authors' collections.*

City Band were frequent happenings in the summertime. The actual bandshell atop a larger structure was built under the direction of Sacca in 1949.

Unfortunately, after Sacca passed away in 1955, the bandstand was all but abandoned. It served as a hangout spot for local hippies who were up to no good, at least according to town leaders, who had the bandstand demolished in 1969. Only the commemorative plaque remains.

Part Three
DOWNTOWN

What is considered to be "downtown" Ocean City includes the Boardwalk up to Fifteenth Street, but it's much more than just the boards. Downtown Ocean City, from the Inlet Park to Seventeenth Street, is the music-blaring rides and arcade games, the public art, snack shops and beach stores on every side street and the charming, historic churches and guest houses that make Ocean City unique.

After you've gotten your fill of the Boardwalk, spend some time wandering the Boardwalk's side streets down to the bayside blocks downtown. You'll find small coffee shops and cafés, utility boxes painted by local artists and even tiny dive bars that could tell you plenty of stories if walls could talk. The treasures downtown are endless.

13

Downtown Dives

O cean City is home to several decades-old dive bars that serve as watering holes for the locals in the off-season and a place for visitors to cool off with a cold drink in the summer. The Purple Moose is a famous dive on the Boardwalk that's well known for its live entertainment, while the Cork Bar and the Bearded Clam have been seated side by side on Wicomico Street since the mid-twentieth century.

When you thinks about Ocean City nightlife over the years, you might conjure up images of Moose Juice at the Purple Moose, all the military/ police/first responder memorabilia hanging on the walls of the Bearded Clam or the dollar bills taped to the ceiling of the Cork Bar. In fact, it

Dolle's Restaurant on Wicomico Street before it became the Cork Bar. *Courtesy of Dolle's Candyland Inc.*

should be noted that those dollar bills at the Cork Bar have raised more than $80,000, as of 2019, for the Autistic Children's Support Group of Worcester County. The tradition started around 2008, when a regular drunkenly stuck his cash to the ceiling of the bar, and it quickly caught on. The bills often fall down, and when they do, they're collected in a donation jar and promptly given to charity.

However, even with all the dive bar watering holes that have served their regulars and summer tourists for decades, there's only one operating bar in Ocean City that's been around since the Prohibition era: Harbor Inn.

HARBOR INN

It's the very definition of a hole-in-the-wall dive bar, but it's hard to miss if you happen to be walking on the bayside at Somerset Street. The music playing from the jukebox can almost always be heard outside the front door, which is usually wide open to present a perfect view of guests playing pool, drinking cheap beer, sitting on spinning vinyl stools and chatting up bartenders.

Summer nights at the Harbor Inn paint a scene that you'd expect from a beach town's downtown dive bar, and most nonregulars who stop in for a pint don't even realize they're sitting in the oldest bar in town.

The Harbor Inn has always been owned by women, since the mid-1920s, when owner Sheree Musson's grandparents, Irish and Emma Farrell, first opened the building as a market. This was during Prohibition, when they couldn't legally sell alcohol, though as bartender Buddy Groff plainly put it, "Trust me, they were selling liquor before Prohibition."

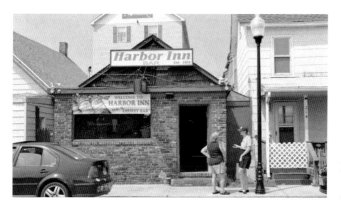

Outside Ocean City's oldest bar, located bayside on Somerset Street. *B.L. Strang-Moya.*

One of Harbor Inn's many unique decorations, a Barbie that was left for bartender Dawn. *B.L. Strang-Moya.*

"Years ago, when my grandmother first opened it up, she was friends with the chief of police," Musson recalled. "It was really originally a little market for the marina over here, and she would pour whiskey in Coca-Cola bottles and put them in the counters where the candy or whatever was sold."

The chief of police would call Musson's grandmother whenever the police had plans to raid the place, and she'd put the illegal Coke bottles in a cart and wheel them around the block until the cops were gone. It pays to have friends in high places.

On close inspection of the Harbor Inn, it's clear that the place has its own host of oddities in its four brick walls. Framed newspaper articles detailing the bar's long life—from Prohibition and beyond—hang above pool tables. Behind the bar are photos of Robert Donaldson, also known as "Fish," a beloved patron and barback of Harbor Inn, who passed away in 2018, next to a signed picture of bartender Buddy with members of the heavy metal band Jackyl, who visited the bar in secret one night when they were passing through town. Half-naked Barbie and Ken dolls sit on top of a television. They were brought in by friends of a bartender named Dawn "to be her boyfriends." One shirtless bleach-blond Ken doll in swim trunks has "Dawn's #1" written in permanent marker across his plastic abs.

Tourists stumble in all summer long, and local regulars keep the taps pouring in the off-season well after most other downtown bars have closed for the year.

14

Freak Street

Back in the 1980s, teenagers used to hang out around First Street near the Trimper's Himalaya, a ride that blasted loud rock music day and night. (Today it plays mostly pop radio hits.) This hangout was dubbed Freak Street, and the concept was as simple as socializing with fellow metalheads and enjoying the music from the blacktop amusement park, where they had to blare the music from the Himalaya's speakers for riders to hear above the relentless spinning and jerking around.

"We could walk up and down or sit on each side of the little street trying to meet people or find a date," remembered one Freak Street regular. "It was also known to some as 'skid row.' Either way, it was a blast for us kids."

"We never allowed popped collar goofs or preppies to hang there," remembered another regular. "They were not cool."

The police department started enforcing anti-loitering laws with a heavier hand at some point in the '90s. Freak Street died around the same time as hair metal.

15

Henry Hotel

The brown-shingled, three-story Henry Hotel sits on the corner of Baltimore and South Division Streets. It's been empty for decades, but it was once a lively hub in the center of downtown known for accommodating acclaimed black musicians, including Cab Calloway, Count Basie and Duke Ellington. "Henry's Colored Hotel," as it was called in the early twentieth century, was one of the few places in town where African American vacationers could stay.

The Henry Hotel was built in 1895 and, in 2019, though vacant, remains on the corner of South Baltimore Avenue. *B.L. Strang-Moya.*

Built around 1895, the hotel was acquired by Charles T. and Louisa Henry in 1926. Back then, the Boardwalk and oceanside beach were off-limits to African Americans, except when Boardwalk merchants would hold "Colored Excursion Days" at the end of the summer season to boost sales.

From the time the Henry was built until the mid-twentieth century, local restaurants and hotels employed black workers but wouldn't allow them to use their facilities. Even big-name musicians who played at the Pier Ballroom, including a young James Brown, were prohibited from staying at segregated hotels. They lodged at the Henry Hotel instead.

The Henry Hotel is the only surviving hotel that hosted African Americans in Ocean City at that time, and it remains under African American ownership today.

16

Ocean Bowl Skate Park

W hen skateboarding really started to take the country by storm in the 1970s, many of the young people of Ocean City took to the craze. Surfing and skating went hand in hand, so naturally, a coastal beach town with a large population of surfers became a breeding ground for Maryland skateboarding.

As more and more skaters took to the side streets, rails and drained wintertime swimming pools of Ocean City, some members of the public grew more and more concerned. Skating was banned by city officials in the early '70s, and there was no proposal to provide a sanctioned area where skating could take place. It was a grassroots moment started by one concerned parent, who has been dubbed the mother of skateboarding in Ocean City, of all skateboarding on the East Coast, even, that led to the development of Ocean Bowl.

Dorothy "Haystack" Marlowe, mother of skateboarding boys in town (who'd also been called "MOSS," Mother of Super Skaters), led other skateboarding supporters to a city council meeting, where they made their plea for the construction of a skate park in town. Jack Crosby, an art teacher at Berlin Middle School, constructed a clay model of the proposed skate park, which he and Marlowe presented at the council meeting.

Their efforts paid off, and in 1976, Ocean Bowl opened its gates to crowds of enthusiastic young skaters. The facility consisted of a four-foot-deep asphalt bowl, and a larger bowl was added soon after. In 1984, the larger bowl had been weathered down by a succession of tropical

A skater takes Ocean Bowl's vert ramp, circa 1987. *Courtesy of Patrick Eisenhauer.*

storms and was replaced by an eleven-foot-tall, twenty-eight-foot-wide metal halfpipe.

"The second version, from 1986 until 1997, is the Ocean Bowl that I knew," recalled Patrick Eisenhauer, a self-proclaimed skate rat, who grew up taking family vacations to Ocean City and spending many long summer days at Ocean Bowl. "The bowl itself was a lumpy amorphous mess. You could roll down the ramp, carve the walls, maybe air out of the center bump, and, if it had a parking block, do a few lip tricks at the top of the bank. It was obviously a left-over from the '70s era. It was fun but also frustrating to try to keep up any speed. I still skated it yearly."

In 1997, more wear and the ever-evolving needs of skaters resulted in another renovation. The old ramp and the original bowl were demolished to make room for the park's newer facilities, which would come to include a vertical ramp, a mini ramp, a beloved Ocean Bowl concrete pool, a small bowl or "bird bath," a Gnar wall, banked walls, a pyramid, corners and hips and escalators—facilities that serve skaters in the park to this day.

Eisenhauer revisited Ocean Bowl in recent years and found the experience enjoyable, if somewhat less lumpy and amorphous than his experiences in the '80s and '90s.

He recounted:

All I really did was carve around, do some ollies, 50-50s and rock 'n' rolls. What's interesting is that it was built in 1998. We are currently in the midst of a huge skate park boom, with vast numbers built in the last five to ten years; 1998 is well ahead of the curve and shows a great deal of forethought, and because of that, Ocean Bowl is still a major destination for skaters. Most of the guys I met there last summer were not on vacation. They had memberships and had driven in from other parts

Skateboarding enthusiast Patrick Eisenhauer at Ocean Bowl, circa 1988. *Courtesy of Patrick Eisenhauer.*

of the state to skate the park. The footprint is still the same as the old Ocean Bowl, on the corner of an empty block, with ball courts next to it and some fields behind it.

The skate park received an uptick in attention and much-needed updates during the Dew Tour's run. Ocean City provided a home for the tour, a multisport event that includes skateboarding, surfing and BMX, from 2011 through 2014. Skaters from all over the country who came to town for the event took advantage of Ocean City's premier skate park. In fact, Dew Tour notwithstanding, passionate skateboarders have made pilgrimages to Ocean City for decades to grind the rails and ride the half-pipe at Ocean Bowl—a rite of passage of sorts for young skaters.

Ocean Bowl is the oldest operating municipal skate park in the United States.

17

The Angler

Just a few blocks down from Ocean Bowl Skate Park is the Angler, positioned on the water at the very end of the Route 50 bridge. Captain Bill Bunting's Angler restaurant opened in 1938. It is likely Ocean City's oldest restaurant. Its current owners, Jayne Bunting Kendall and Julie Bunting Smith, are the fourth generation of Buntings to operate the restaurant and marina.

Charles Rollins Bunting purchased the Angler's property in the 1930s—back when the plot of land was only marsh grass and before the inlet provided nearby access to the Atlantic. There was no dock yet. In fact, the Buntings were the first family in Ocean City to be issued a dock building permit. Bunting owned all of the property south of where the Angler currently stands. He gave each of his five sons a parcel of land and put them in competition with each other as they opened their own restaurants and marinas.

One son, William Bunting, erected a small building adjoining his father's dock, where he sold fishing bait and sodas and rented out small boats. His wife, Louise, started selling homemade pies, and then breakfast, to the fishermen before they headed out for the day.

"There wasn't Wawa or Royal Farms and all those places to stop then," Jayne said. "So, they came to this destination, where she had coffee for them, and she started making things for them to have to take on the boat."

Business picked up after the inlet was formed, but Captain Bunting and his boat, the *Angler*, were called to serve in the coast guard in World War II.

When he returned home, Bunting found that storms had washed the dock away, and in 1945, a new dock and addition were built.

A tradition of constant updating and refurbishing the business has continued since the Angler's early years. After Hurricane Sandy bombarded the East Coast in 2012, the Angler underwent a "total rehab," much like the necessary reconstruction it endured back in 1945.

The Angler, restaurant and fishing charter, are testaments to old Ocean City and the resilience of some seaside businesses in town. Times change and storms roll through, but some traditions hold up, even after eighty-one years.

18

Beach Birds

I n the spring of 2003, eighty-two new birds made their debut in Ocean City, among the hundreds of thousands (perhaps millions) of seagulls who already call the Maryland coast their home in the summertime. These birds were notable because they stood five feet tall and were made of fiberglass, and they were refreshing because, unlike their smaller warm-blooded counterparts, they didn't try to steal anyone's fries or deliver surprises from the sky at unsuspecting beachgoers' heads.

Each beach bird was made by a Canadian craftsman and was conceptualized and painted by local artists. They were displayed all over town, from the Boardwalk to the inside of city hall and local restaurants and hotels, before they were auctioned off to fund future public art projects and exhibits in Ocean City.

Lauren Taylor, the local business owner who headed the beach bird project, called it an "entertaining and unstuffy" way to bring art downtown. The birds provided a whimsical splash of color and local flavor wherever they appeared, making art accessible and enjoyable to people from all walks of life.

Every bird was different, to say the least. Some were puns, some were quirky and all of them were undoubtedly eye catching. They were often topical—the shamrock bird proudly represented Shenanigans Irish Pub on 4th Street and the Boardwalk, and down a block on 3rd Street, the dough-dough bird drew intrigued patrons into the Dough Roller. Birdwalk Elvis paid tribute to Ocean City's most beloved Boardwalk character, famously

Two remaining beach birds stand outside the Art League of Ocean City in 2017—the bird dog, which has since been repainted, and one adorned with pieces of glass and musical notes. *Kristin Helf.*

portrayed by the late Norman Webb. The jailbird stood guard outside the police station. And Jonathan Livingston Beagull, who lived on 120th Street, was one of the most memorable for having a dog head attached seamlessly to its bird body.

Businesses, individuals and sectors of the local government covered the cost of the birds, which totaled at $170,000. Unpainted birds were $750, while painted birds were $1,000.

The project was inspired by some of the public art that was already on display in Ocean City—namely, the white marlin sculpture at the foot of the Route 50 bridge. A few of the birds can still be found hiding at select public locations in Ocean City, but most of them now reside in private homes and backyards.

19
Modern Monuments

BEACH BALL WATER TOWER

It's a bird; it's a plane; it's a blue, white, green, orange and red beach ball in the sky that never hits the ground. Ocean City's beach ball water tower is a newly famous but already iconic modern monument that signals to beachgoers traveling in caravans piled high with plastic pails and sunscreen as they cross the Route 50 bridge that their summer vacation has finally begun.

The beach ball tower as it stood in the summer of 2019. *B.L. Strang-Moya.*

Construction on the First Street water tower began in June 2015, and it wasn't until November 2017 that it was complete. The new, freshly painted landmark replaced two aging water towers on Worcester and Fifteenth Streets and resulted in improved water quality and distribution and reduced maintenance costs. The project, funded by general obligation bonds, cost approximately $4.9 million.

The beach ball tower holds one million gallons of water and was built by Chicago Bridge and Iron Inc., subcontractors with the Town of Ocean City. When conceptualizing the water tower's design, the mayor and city council discussed simply painting the tower with the town's logo but ultimately decided to spend the extra $10,000 it would take to cover the landmark in the bright, memorable beach ball design.

WHITE MARLIN FOUNTAIN

Across the way from the big beach ball in Entry Park is the white marlin fountain, which serves as Ocean City's unofficial welcome committee and is one of the first things that visitors see when they're spit off of the Route 50 bridge and onto the peninsula. Since the marlin was created and displayed jumping out of a big brick fountain in 2002, it's also represented a title that Ocean City continues to earn summer after summer: the white marlin capital of the world.

Crafted by artist Paul Lockhart, the white marlin fountain has greeted visitors as they exit the Route 50 bridge since 2002. *B.L. Strang-Moya.*

It was President Franklin Roosevelt who first deemed Ocean City the world's white marlin capital after a particularly prosperous day of fishing at the inlet in 1939. Since 1974, Ocean City has hosted the world's largest billfish tournament, known as the White Marlin Open, where payouts to champion fishermen have run well into million-dollar territory in recent years.

Paul Lockhart, a metal artist based on the Eastern Shore of Maryland, created the white marlin sculpture. The project was funded by the Ocean City Downtown Corporation (OCDC), a nonprofit dedicated to the revitalization of downtown. Fishermen who visit every August for the famed White Marlin Open might be exhilarated upon seeing the fifteen-foot stainless steel marlin fountain. Or, they may only be reminded of the ineluctable challenges of the competition, consisting of equal parts skill, luck and tenacity.

DANCE OF THE DOLPHINS

The white marlin sculpture isn't the town's only artistic dedication to marine life. Similar to the marlin at the foot of the Route 50 bridge, the *Dance of the Dolphins* sculpture greets visitors who enter from the Route 90 bridge, providing three friendly faces who represent one of the most beloved mammals in the Atlantic Ocean.

Unlike the other two entry points to Ocean City, there was no public art at the terminus of the Route 90 bridge to provide a spark of whimsy and welcome for families driving into town. OCDC proposed the dolphin statue to the mayor and city council in 2014, and it wasn't long before the new public art project was off the ground.

The sculpture features three bronze dolphins that measure five, seven and eight feet in height—nine feet total—and sit on an eight-foot bronze base. The dancing dolphins debuted in the spring of 2015. The sculpture is mounted in its own plaza at the corner of Route 90 and Coastal Highway and was funded by donations. Three families who each donated $10,000 to the project were given the opportunity to name the dolphins; their names are Haven Hunter, Clearwater and Summer.

The artist who crafted the dancing dolphins, David Turner of Onley, Virginia, also crafted the *Spillin' the Wind* eagle statue, which greets visitors from Delaware on 144th Street. *Spillin' the Wind* was completed in 2007.

At the foot of the Route 90 bridge is the *Dance of the Dolphins* sculpture, designed by David Turner and unveiled in 2015. Both the white marlin fountain and the *Dance of the Dolphins* sculpture are public art projects organized by Ocean City Development Corporation. *B.L. Strang-Moya.*

FIREFIGHTER'S MEMORIAL

Another of Ocean City's famous monuments erected in the 2000s, the firefighter's memorial on Caroline Street and the Boardwalk is a tribute to the Ocean City firefighters of past and present, as well as the 343 New York City firefighters who lost their lives on September 11, 2001.

The discussion surrounding a potential monument to honor Ocean City's dedicated firefighters began in the mid-1990s, but the idea never made it far off the ground. The estimated costs of the project were enough to see that the monument never made it out of the initial idea phase.

In the early 2000s, several of the fire department's more prominent members passed away. People made donations to the department in their memory, and with those new funds, the memorial project was reborn. On September 11, 2006, the five-year anniversary of 9/11, the statue debuted in its place on the Boardwalk, framed by five flags—the American flag, the Maryland flag, the Worcester County flag, the Ocean City flag and a Fire and Rescue Service flag—waving high above the ground.

The bronze statue depicts a six-foot-tall firefighter standing on a black granite block inscribed with three dedications—one to the firefighters of the world, one to the New York City Fire Department and one to the Ocean City firefighters of the past, present and future.

In a smaller granite block next to the firefighter is a twisted piece of steel recovered from the World Trade Center. "We will never forget," the accompanying plaque reads.

The firefighter's memorial on the Boardwalk was erected on September 11, 2006, the five-year anniversary of 9/11. *Kristin Helf.*

Part Four
MIDTOWN–NORTH OCEAN CITY

Motels, mini golf and a whole other world of amusements extend beyond the offerings of the downtown region. From midtown Ocean City, starting around 17th Street, up to North Ocean City, ending where Fenwick Island, Delaware, begins at 146th Street, Ocean City makes a name for itself aside from the Boardwalk and the bustling downtown.

While downtown Ocean City doesn't always go to sleep at night, Ocean City's upper streets are often thought of as the more family- and retiree-friendly section of town. But that doesn't mean it is without its own host of oddities—quite the contrary.

20

Old Pro Golf Today and Yesterday

About as familiar as the smell of funnel cake and the sound of the crashing waves on the beach is the thrill visitors feel when they spot an Old Pro Miniature Golf sign on Coastal Highway. The great American pastime of miniature golf is not uncommon in resort towns, but the Old Pro Golf courses, cherished by locals and tourists, happen to be an extraordinary assemblage of the most fun-to-play and well-produced courses in the country.

Old Pro was founded in 1963, just one year after the Great March Storm of 1962, by Herbert and Aileen Schoellkopf. They were experts in the industry and had been successful in operating other courses and amusement centers along the East Coast. In all, Herbert dedicated more than seventy years to designing, engineering, constructing and managing over 150 miniature golf courses.

The Old Pro courses are memorable for their themed environments, creative designs using three-dimensional molded figures—most of them hand-sculpted from fiberglass and often animated—and challenging hole designs with no shortage of obstacles, including water features. Imaginative landscaping and well-kept gardens along the greens are also hallmarks of an Old Pro course. It's said that Herbert was an avid gardener.

Many Old Pro courses have come and gone over the years, lining the Ocean City landscape with kitschy roadside oddities and obstacles since the first two courses—one Western and one outer space themed—made their debuts on the pier in 1963 and operated until 1978. One of the courses on the pier was later overhauled to a sports theme and became

Top and middle: Old Pro Golf Pirate Course in 1985. *John Margolies/ Library of Congress.*

Bottom: Treasure Hunt Golf in 1985. *John Margolies/Library of Congress.*

Old Pro Golf on the Pier, circa 1967. *Courtesy of Earl Shores.*

famous for including Baltimore Colts quarterback Johnny Unitas as an obstacle. Shortly after, a Polynesian-themed course opened on Twenty-Third Street.

The late 1960s and early 1970s saw the creation of multiple courses up and down Coastal Highway. All the while, Old Pro Golf was booming in nearby states, including New Jersey, Delaware and South Carolina, with upward of fifteen other courses in operation—some for other clients who hired Herbert for his artistic services. In all, Herbert owned and operated twenty locations from New Jersey to South Carolina. Today, all of his courses have closed except for those located in Ocean City.

In 1994, Herbert introduced his first indoor, all-weather, air-conditioned course behind his 68th Street dinosaur location. He later built a second indoor location on 136th Street themed as the "Undersea Adventure," while simultaneously reimagining three of his outdoor courses also at that location.

Herbert Schoellkopf passed away in May 2016, but his legacy lives on in the resort. The family-owned-and-operated Old Pro business continues thanks to the dedication of his family members and employees. As of 2019, visitors can enjoy the Old Pro experience at four locations housing

Clockwise from top left: Old Pro Basketball Player in 1986; Old Pro Circus Course in 1985; Sunburst Golf in 1985; Jungle Golf in 1985. *John Margolies/Library of Congress.*

six courses, including Temple of the Dragon on 23rd Street, Renaissance Castle on 28th Street, Indoor Undersea Adventure and Prehistoric Dinosaur on 68th Street and Indoor Safari Village and Caribbean Pirates on 136th Street.

21

Anthony's Dancing Liquors

For those heading north on Coastal Highway, Thirty-Third Street marks the home of the venerable Anthony's Liquors, which dates back well over a half century. A robust selection of beer, wine and liquor; a deli; and a twenty-five-seat, full-service bar with convenient access from Coastal Highway make the establishment one of the town's most favorited locales. Despite its offerings, the iconic sign on the building's façade is what will be most indelible in the minds of tourists and locals.

The "dancing" sign is a simple concept—two beer cans and a wine bottle blissfully arm in arm, dancing the night away. Thanks to fancy neon work, the legs of the characters are animated and make the sign undeniably charming.

The dancing liquor bottles sign at Anthony's Liquors on Thirty-Third Street has made the shop immediately recognizable during the day or night since the 1970s.
Karl Schwartz.

The sign's original concept was the brainchild of the store's owner, Jon Christ, who, between 1965 and today, has expanded the shop several times from a small drive-up store to the full-service liquor store, deli and bar that sits on the corner today. The first iteration of the sign in the 1970s was a simple, hand-painted version of the dancing cans on plywood, which hung on the south side of the building. When the business expanded in 1982, Christ had the sign overhauled by the Selby Sign Company out of Pocomoke City to include the backlit characters and neon animation that many people still find so amusing.

Many people credit the Anthony's sign as being one of their earliest memories of vacationing in Ocean City, and others consider it their favorite sign in town. A little humor, creativity and ingenuity—not to mention a lot of history—go a long way.

22

Motel Row

From the inlet to Fifteenth Street, most accommodations in Ocean City are touted for their gorgeous oceanfront or sweeping bayside views, along with other perks like Boardwalk access, continental breakfast and state-of-the-art gym facilities. From Thirty-Third Street north, it's much of the same but without the Boardwalk access because the Boardwalk ends at Twenty-Seventh Street.

But between Fifteenth and Thirty-Third Streets, amenities and proximity to local landmarks and things to do take a backseat, at least for a minute, when one first lays eyes on Motel Row. What is immediately apparent is that these few oceanside blocks are more of a time machine than anything else in Ocean City.

After World War II, motels gained a huge market share of tourism in the United States and offered travelers inexpensive lodging. These travelers could pull their cars right up to the door and spend a night or two in an air-conditioned room. Sometimes the rooms would even come equipped with a color television or the class and comfort of a Magic Fingers vibrating bed.

The motel industry peaked in 1964, with sixty-one thousand motels operating throughout the country. By 2012, however, there were only sixteen thousand motel properties still in commission.

The first properties to hit Ocean City's Motel Row—the Sea Scape, the Surf and Sands, the Santa Maria and the Stowaway—were built in the mid-1950s and, unfortunately, have since been replaced with newer

Top: One of the most iconic motels of Motel Row, the Flamingo Motel, opened its original, twenty-three-unit building in 1963. *Kristin Helf.*

Bottom: Ocean Lanes, Ocean City's only bowling alley, has been a tradition for local bowling leagues and kids celebrating birthdays since September 11, 1966. *Authors' collections.*

accommodations. However, a number of motels built soon after those original four are still standing.

While motels aren't nearly as in demand as they once were, Ocean City still holds a lion's share of beauteous retro, mid-century modern/ art deco–style motels that remain open for business today, at least in the summertime.

The Flamingo Motel, at the north end of Motel Row on Thirty-First Street, has been owned and operated by the same family since 1963. When George Brous first opened the motel, it consisted of one twenty-three-unit building. As of 2019, the second-generation business operates three ocean block buildings and is well known for its iconic neon sign, featuring the words "Flamingo Motel" and its namesake bird illuminated in pink. It's iconic, but it's not the only sign of its kind; in fact, it's hard to drive down Motel Row at night without counting all the vintage, neon motel signs lighting up the sky.

The Ocean Mecca on Twenty-Third Street was built in 1958 by William and Kathleen Harman to provide a sort of oasis to travelers. The Arabian style of the motel's sign and exterior pay homage to some of Kathleen Harman's favorite movies, *The Sheik* and *The Voyages of Sinbad*.

On Nineteenth Street is the Empress Motel. Built in 1965, the Empress still has its original neon peacock sign, as the peacock is the sign of royalty in many cultures.

Other mid-century motels include the Seabonay, with its loopy, cursive sign jutting from the rooftop high in the air; the angular, seafoam blue Eden Roc; the Thunderbird; the Sahara; and the Safari. On its Boardwalk-facing rooftop balcony, a large gorilla statue peers down and guards the Safari.

THE SEA SCAPE AND PEPPER'S TAVERN

By Karl Schwarz

The Sea Scape Motel, built on Sixteenth Street in 1954 by Ridge Harman, was Ocean City's first Boardwalk motel. It advanced the era when the Chesapeake Bay Bridge eased access to Ocean City and catered to the more casual atmosphere sought by families bringing their baby boomer children to the beach. The Sea Scape closed after the 2016 season and was replaced by the Hyatt Place Hotel, which opened in fall 2018.

Pepper's Tavern operated in the basement of the Sea Scape Motel for almost twenty years. Dennis "Denny-O" King arrived in Ocean City in 1979 and worked in several businesses, including arcade game operations. While servicing his machines at the Sea Scape's Tavern by the Sea, the tavern's owner suggested Denny-O buy the business, and Pepper's Tavern was born. Pepper's bar food menu, low ceilings, underground location and walls covered with the handwritten names of thousands of customers who successfully consumed a plate of their scorching "Hell Wings" made Pepper's a true dive. That fact, plus its solid food menu and loyal customer base, led to Denny-O calling Pepper's the "Finest Five-Star Dive." The phrase stuck and became Pepper's recognized moniker. Denny-O died in 2014, but Pepper's remained in business until just a few days before the Sea Scape motel was demolished.

A modest sign outside of Pepper's Tavern, which operated out of the basement of the Sea Scape Motel until 2016. *Karl Schwarz*.

23

Bobby Baker's Carousel

High-rise condos and hotels now stretch as far as the eye can see, cascading down Coastal Highway from midtown Ocean City and north toward Delaware. But long before the sweeping city skyline of North Ocean City, before there was more than the dunes and the occasional mom-and-pop shop, there was Bobby Baker's Carousel.

The carousel, now a sky-grazing oceanfront hotel and condominium building on 118th Street, is also a relic of mid-century Ocean City that has withstood the test of time and helped paved the way for the town's north end. It was a trendsetter, and it was not without its share of controversy.

Originally called Bobby Baker's Carousel Motel, the building opened in July 1962, standing at only four stories high and able to host 250 people at a time. The beachfront plot of land was purchased in 1959 for $75,000—not a bad deal for an oceanside property, but that was a time when Ocean City only extended as far as Forty-First Street. Commotion and excitement surrounded the grand opening of the carousel, but many wondered why a $1.2 million structure would be built in what was still practically Fenwick Island, Delaware.

In its heyday, the carousel was host to a revolving door of politicians and Washington elites. Bobby Baker himself, the original owner of the hotel, was an adviser to Lyndon B. Johnson and served as secretary to the Democratic majority leader in 1953. Johnson and his wife famously pulled up to the carousel at its grand opening in a sparkling limousine, among other guests from Washington, D.C.

A vintage postcard from the Carousel Motel, which opened in 1962. *Authors' collections.*

In an article titled "Bobby Baker's Carousel: Reminiscences of a Small Town," an unnamed political insider said, "In D.C...the prevailing view at the time was that LBJ himself tasked Bobby with building the Carousel expressly for the purpose of making a hideaway where Washington pols could conduct their personal business outside the microscope of the D.C. press corps and others." Baker denied this. The *Coastal Style* article details the life and times of Baker in Ocean City, his political life marred by scandal, a romantic escapade ending in a plane crash, mysterious business dealings and a little about the early history of the hotel. In short, it's a doozy.

When Baker went to prison in 1971 for bribery, tax evasion and fraud, his wife and brother-in-law sold the hotel out from under him, much to Baker's dismay. The family eventually faded into obscurity, and most of the theatrics surrounding the carousel and its owners would be relegated to the history books.

It's been a long journey from a four-story motel standing alone in the great, empty expanse of North Ocean City and serving as a respite for high-power Washingtonians to one of Ocean City's most famous high-rises. Today, the original building remains on the east side of the twenty-two-story hotel that was built in 1974.

The carousel is one business of many that helped shape Ocean City into the resort town that we know and love today. It was once the northernmost outpost and would pave the way for other condos, hotels and development in North Ocean City as a whole.

24

The Muffler Man Pirate

S tep back in time with this 1964 advertisement from the International
Fiberglass Company (IFC) out of Venice, California, which featured
many large figures produced by the company, some of which were, and
still are, displayed in town. The most recognizable and widely used product
produced by IFC was the large, bearded "salesman," who stood twenty
feet tall, weighed nearly four hundred pounds and was often distinguished
by his right palm facing up and left palm facing down, generally grasping
something relevant to the business being advertised.

The Muffler Man Pirate. *Authors' collections.*

A 1964 advertisement for the Muffler Man Pirate, referred to here as the "Giant Salesman," from the International Fiberglass Company. *Authors' collections.*

These figures, often referred to as "Muffler Men," were installed all over the country in various applications (mostly automotive businesses and later junkyards) and twice in Ocean City—at the entrance to Ocean Playland Amusement Park, which closed in 1980, on Sixty-Fifth Street near the monorail (originally outfitted as a pirate an later as a clown), and another that is still in use as a sword-wielding pirate at the entrance of Jolly Roger Amusement Park.

25

Gone but Not Forgotten

SIXTY-FIFTH STREET SLIDE 'N RIDE

The summer of 1976 was an exciting time in midtown thanks to the opening of the Sixty-Fifth Street Slide 'N Ride complex, which included an iconic thirty-foot-tall hilltop water slide and later a miniature golf course, bumper boats, batting cages, a basketball court and ample rides and amusements for children.

The park was behind the Sixty-Fourth Street shopping center and was only a stone's throw away from Ocean Playland Amusement Park. In fact, the Slide 'N Ride's sign along Coastal Highway originally belonged to Playland before it closed, and the sign was repurposed.

Visible from the highway were the park's three iconic blue water slides nestled into the artificial hillside, which comprised roughly forty thousand cubic yards of fill dirt and cost about $200,000 to build. The top of the man-made hill was the highest land elevation in Ocean City. The cleverly named slides included the King Kiddie Slide, Sui Slide and Katie Slide, all of which emptied into ground-level splash pools. Generally, it took fifteen seconds to slide down the hill and thirty to walk back up, allowing kids to get a good forty slides in during a half hour on the hill. Large closed-cell foam mats were the main vessel for transporting customers down the smooth-troweled concrete slide painted sky blue. For those who wanted to stay dry, the thriving fleet of nineteen water boats were popular with the older crowd, while the kiddie boats were perfect for children between the ages of two and

What remained of the Slide 'N Ride sign along Coastal Highway in 2008. *Brandon Seidl.*

Deserted miniature golf after the park closed. The thirty-foot-tall hilltop water slide can be seen in the background. *Brandon Seidl.*

The bumper boats have been pulled ashore and abandoned. The pumps that circulate water to the top of the water slides have been permanently turned off and retired. *Brandon Seidl.*

seven. A nautical-themed miniature golf course, five batting cages and Bank Shot Basketball for children were all memorable mainstays on summer days.

The summer of 2008 witnessed the last smile and heard the last laugh coming from atop the hill. After thirty-three summers in operation, the owner decided to turn in the keys and enjoy retirement. Demolition occurred during September 2008, and most of the equipment on the land was sold privately or stored, revealing a bare property that was merely the shell of what it once was. In due time, the site would be demolished and the hill leveled, with the land eventually becoming a parking and storage lot for the city. The slide was believed to be oldest water slide in Maryland when it closed.

PLANET MAZE

Located on Coastal Highway on Thirty-Third Street from 1995 to 2018, Planet Maze was famous for its giant green alien structures that guarded the golf course and for being an exceptionally popular spot for local kids

Planet Maze just days before it was demolished in late 2018. *Kristin Helf.*

to have their birthday parties. The outer space–themed amusement center was a competitor with the Old Pro courses but was about as iconic during its twenty-four-year tenure in Ocean City.

Planet Maze, which consisted of the Lasertron laser tag area, Lost Galaxy outdoor mini golf and a climbing maze, first opened its doors in 1995. Much to the dismay of children, nostalgic young adults and science fiction and mini golf enthusiasts, Planet Maze would see its last Putt-Putt in October 2018. Rina Thaler, who owned Planet Maze with her husband, Jeff Thaler, and couple Jamie and Jeff Albright, cited their children growing up and moving away as one of the reasons why they decided it was time to close the business.

"It's time for us to move on," she said. "It's been a wonderful thing for our families and everyone who has visited there."

GOLD RUSH TERRITORY

The 1980s witnessed rapid expansion in North Ocean City, and while everyone enjoyed the conveniences of housing and restaurants popping up out of the sand, it was still lacking entertainment in the way of classic amusements that the downtown area had enjoyed for a century prior.

That is, until 1982, when Charles "Buddy" Jenkins, owner of the town's popular Jolly Roger amusement enterprise, opened Gold Rush Territory on 125th Street. Gold Rush was a dazzling amusement center that offered a little bit of everything, including miniature golf, bumper boats and a full arcade. It was situated next to Granny's Gold Rush Pizza and Beer, an

Top, left: Native American in Gold Rush Territory, 1985. *John Margolies/Library of Congress.*

Top, right: Cowboy boot in Gold Rush Territory, 1985. *John Margolies/Library of Congress.*

Bottom, right: Granny's Gold Rush Pizza and Beer in 1985. Located on 125th Street with the rest of Jolly Roger's Gold Rush Territory, including mini golf, bumper boats and an arcade, Granny's nourished its guests from 1982 to the early 1990s. *John Margolies/Library of Congress.*

Bottom, left: Granny's Gold Rush arcade coin, circa 1980s. *Brandon Seidl.*

eating establishment for those who craved a slice of pie or a few beverages before teeing off.

The property was outfitted with beautiful landscaping reminiscent of the gold rush era—cactus, stone walkways, sand and pebble gardens and a rustling waterfall that drained into a lagoon that was nestled in the middle of the golf course. The holes were challenging, and there was no shortage of eye-catching obstacles around the course, including a twenty-foot-tall fiberglass Native American statue, an eight-foot-tall cowboy boot and numerous totem poles, tepees, buffalo and relics from the Old West, reminding us of years past. The back portion of the course ascended to a hill, which served as a nice backdrop to the complex from Coastal Highway.

Close to Coastal Highway, in front of the miniature golf course, existed another body of water—this one used for bumper boats. It was a ritual for riders to get soaked while circling the water arena with their pals, and for most, it was a welcome end to a hot summer day. Since the boats were gas-powered back then, speed was never a concern.

For those who wanted to stay in the air conditioning, there was never a dull moment inside the arcade. One of the few largescale video game venues in the North, there was no shortage of classic video, redemption and skill games for young and old. As it was part of the pizza shop, kids would often spend hours playing, eating and socializing during the summer.

Gold Rush Territory quietly shut down in 1998, and in 1999, the large bodies of water were permanently filled in as the property underwent redevelopment to include a new Dough Roller restaurant and, later, Dough Roller Mini Golf. Today, Nick's Mini Golf and Grotto Pizza sit on the property.

In late 1981, Jenkins got approval from the city council to build a scenic go-cart attraction called "Cumberland Trail" just south of the Gold Rush Territory; however, it was never built for reasons unknown.

OCEAN PLAYLAND

In 1965, construction was completed on Ocean Playland Amusement Park with a price tag of more than $2 million on Sixty-Fifth Street bayside, on a large peninsular lot that protruded into the bay. The park was only 860 feet long and 375 feet wide and sat behind a one-thousand-car parking lot off of Coastal Highway.

It officially opened for its first day of business on June 18, 1965, was developed by realtors Jim Caine, Oscar Carey and George Chandler and

Above: A wide-angle view of Ocean Playland. *Courtesy of Earl Shores.*

Middle: The Muffler Man Pirate at Ocean Playland. *Courtesy of Earl Shores.*

Bottom: An ad for Ocean Playland. *Courtesy of Earl Shores.*

OCEAN PLAYLAND
65th St., On The Bay
OCEAN CITY'S ONLY ROLLER COASTER
Thrill To The MONORAIL TRAIN & SKYRIDE
Free Admission - Free Parking for 1000 Cars
OPEN WEEKDAYS - SAT. & SUN.
at 5 PM   at Noon

Ocean Playland monorail advertisement. *Courtesy of Earl Shores.*

was built to offer amusements to those staying in uptown Ocean City. It became an immediate success in North Ocean City, which, at the time, was extremely underdeveloped and sparse.

Ocean Playland, as the park was originally named, was later rebranded as simply "Playland." It operated as a concessionaire park—businessmen and women would come from all over to set up their equipment and pay a percentage of their earnings to the park as a concession.

Unlike many of its competitors, Ocean Playland offered a pay-one-price riding system, so customers could enjoy a plethora of unique attractions, including a complete monorail, a full wooden coaster called the Hurricane, a miniature golf course and dozens of amusement attractions of all types for all ages.

Ocean Playland's Ghost Ship

One of the most significant attractions in Ocean Playland was the Ghost Ship, a dark ride built by Bill Tracy, who at the time worked under a company called Universal Design Limited. Although the park closed in

1980, the Ghost Ship would live on in Ocean City for decades to come, thanks to a high bid and a vision from Granville D. Trimper. Granville was able to purchase the ride's contents, including the cars and track, for a later expansion of the Haunted House.

A NOTE FROM CAPTAIN Brandon: In all of my years researching dark rides, Trimper's Rides, and Ocean City, I have never had a greater urge than to solve the mystery of Ocean Playland's Ghost Ship dark ride. It's a defunct attraction that has very limited memorabilia or public information in the form of photos or videos.

My passion for Trimper's Haunted House fueled my interest in the Ghost Ship because of Granville's achievement of incorporating its contents, built by Bill Tracy, into the Haunted House in the late 1980s. The last decade of rigorous searches of information relating to Ocean Playland's Ghost Ship had left me at many dead ends, until a longtime Trimper employee uncovered a small pile of photos found in a tiny cubbyhole in the late Granville Trimper's desk. From this, many Ghost Ship mysteries were solved.

Ghost Ship was a unique dark ride that offered its patrons a random, nautical-themed ride experience. The façade towered above the midway and included a giant skull with crab legs that glared down at passersby. Other props, including a ship and seaweed cutouts, could also be seen on the second-story balcony.

Unlike many other dark ride attractions of the era, Ghost Ship's façade was impressive and had an enormous amount of detail. Giant letters spelled out the ride's name just below the balcony railing. In 1967, Tracy built a nearly identical façade for a Ghost Ship dark ride at Kennywood Park in Pittsburgh, Pennsylvania.

An Ocean Playland advertisement from the 1977 Ocean City guidebook. *Authors' collections.*

139

Above: Remnants of the original Ghost Ship cars as they appeared behind a Trimper warehouse in 2008. *Brandon Seidl.*

Middle: Bill Tracy's now-closed Ghost Ship dark ride at defunct Ocean Playland Amusement Park in 1981. *Trimper's Rides Archive.*

Bottom: Remnants of Bill Tracy's Seasick Pirate stunt as it appeared in Ghost Ship in 1981. *Trimper's Rides Archive.*

Remnants of Bill Tracy's Crab stunt as it appeared in Ghost Ship in 1981. *Trimper's Rides Archive.*

Although it contained different stunts, it was a similar ride that was unfortunately lost to a fire in 1975.

If the façade wasn't enough to make you fall overboard, the lobby area was just as incredible. Bill Tracy's murals of underwater scenery covered the walls and prepared riders for their trip into the abyss. Although Ghost Ship lived a short life of only sixteen years, the two-story building was built out of cinderblock to withstand the harsh Atlantic storms.

THE PADDOCK MARTINI GLASS

People always knew they were on the party block when they spied the big martini glass through their windshield as they drove up Coastal Highway.

The martini glass stood on the corner of Seventeenth Street atop the Paddock's pool bar from 2003 through 2014. The Paddock was once a popular nightclub in Ocean City. Its reign started in 1953, but when the Paddock was replaced with a Western-themed club, Cowboy Coast, in 2014, its iconic martini glass came down with it.

The glass stood twenty-five feet tall and was supposedly filled with sour apple (though how much is unclear because no one knows exactly

Paddock martini glass. *Courtesy of Karl Schwarz.*

how many gallons a twenty-five-foot martini glass can hold), stuck with a straw and garnished with a lime. By 2012, Cîroc's brand name was been printed on the side, though the glass was once blank and unbranded. The structure was built by Kent Signs in Dover, Delaware.

CAP'N BOB'S BULL

"Our Future's So Bright, the Bull's Gotta Wear Shades" was once the catchphrase for midtown Ocean City's iconic bull statue that stood on the corner of Sixty-Fourth Street outside of Captain Bob's Steak and Seafood House. The bull served as a clever advertisement for the establishment's

"Best Slow Roasted Prime Rib" and was a beloved and memorable landmark that still has people talking to this day.

Installed in the mid-1970s, until the restaurant closed in 2003, the monumental fiberglass character, measuring twelve feet tall and twenty feet long and weighing more than a half ton, charmingly greeted those cruising up and down Coastal Highway, wearing a chef's hat, bib and oversized sunglasses.

After Captain Bob's closed, the bull mascot was moved and displayed by Maria's Family Restaurant in Chincoteague, Virginia, for several years. It was then stored nearby and mostly forgotten until its purchase in 2018 by the Parsons family, who had it restored and installed outside their family farm and business, Parsons Farms Produce in Dagsboro, Delaware.

Top: Captain Bob's Bull up close in 1985, back when it stood outside Captain Bob's Steak and Seafood House on Sixty-Fourth Street. *John Margolies/Library of Congress.*

Bottom: Captain Bob's Bull in 1985. *John Margolies/Library of Congress.*

Part Five
WEST OCEAN CITY

Across the Sinepuxent Bay from Ocean City proper is West Ocean City, Maryland—not quite on the peninsula but still very much a part of the culture and tourism industry of the town. Many travelers come barreling down Route 50 and only pass through West Ocean City on their way to the barrier island, but others opt to lodge on the mainland, which is a bit quieter but still just as fun.

West O, as it's often called, is home to fishing charters and marinas, bayside dining, outlet shops and residential communities, along with a long-buried sailor, a Western-themed amusement park and the remnants of an abandoned drive-in theater.

26

Captain Carhart's Grave

There is only one known marked grave in the Ocean City area, located north of the Route 50 bridge in West Ocean City. The grave resides in the boundaries of a housing development on Golf Course Road in Captain's Hill. There are no cemeteries or even another marked tombstone in Ocean City; burying the deceased in a coastal area has long been an unsound idea because shorelines are known to erode, and the grounds of Ocean City have never been conducive to a proper burial. In fact, coastal cemeteries have been known to literally fall into the sea. Historically, most of Ocean City's deceased have been buried in Berlin, Maryland.

The one known marked grave in Ocean City is located far enough from the shore and on an elevated piece of land, which has allowed it to remain for 217 years and counting, though it's unknown if a body even lies underneath. The marble tombstone memorializes Captain William Carhart, a shipwrecked sailor whose vessel sank off the coast of Ocean City in January 1799.

The epitaph reads:

In Memory of
Capt. William Carhart
Shipwrecked off this coast
January 5, 1799
Aged 38 years and
5 months

Captain Carhart's grave in 2019. *B.L. Strang-Moya.*

Next to the tombstone is a smaller footstone engraved with the Captain's initials, *W.C.* There's also a large, rusted anchor that sits on concrete embedded in the ground just a few feet away.

Carhart was from Philadelphia, Pennsylvania. A "Camphene Club of Philadelphia" would reportedly visit the gravesite in the late nineteenth century, where a German band would play songs of mourning, and barrels of beer would be poured out in the late captain's (or possibly a different late unknown sailor's) honor, according to an unofficial account from the *Democratic Messenger* in 1955.

The tombstone was once hidden under the cover of trees before the houses at Captain's Hill were built. In 1991, Suzanne Hurley, the late curator and historian of the Ocean City Life-Saving Station Museum, compiled a feature of three articles that documented the legend and lore of Captain Carhart in Ocean City, which includes the account from the *Democratic Messenger*.

Another article, by Gerald W. Johnson, in the *Evening Sun* in September 1932, described the area of the burial site before all of the development, back when the neighboring golf course was the nearest sign of life and golfers would occasionally stumble upon the grave when they teed off with a little too much vigor.

"A golfer has no right to know about that tombstone," Johnson said. "As you stand on number one tee, you have fifty yards of perfectly clear fairway to the right of the three trees; and that is where you ought to hit your drive. But if you are a duffer, struggling against a mean hook, it is odds on that right into those trees is where you will snap your first shot. And then, as you poke about in some myrtle bushes under the trees, wondering where the deleted-by-censor-the-omitted-fore-propriety thing has got to, you are apt to uncover an upright marble slab."

Captain Carhart's grave and a giant rusted anchor in 2019. *B.L. Strang-Moya.*

Captain Bunting claimed that a drowned Carhart washed ashore in Ocean City after the ship wrecked and that the sailor was initially buried on the beach, but "they got to figuring that if a high tide came and uncovered him they'd be in a bad fix, because he would come back and haunt 'em," which is how he ended up buried in the woods of what is now Captain's Hill.

The stories and legends surrounding Captain Carhart, his crew and the shipwreck differ in myriad ways. Even the date of the shipwreck, inscribed on the tombstone, has been reported differently in oral tradition and in publication.

In "Footnotes to a Legend," by shipwreck researcher Joan D. Charles, Charles reported an article she discovered in the *Philadelphia Daily Advertiser*, dated January 21, 1799, which stated that Carhart's ship was the *Hawk*, not the *Ocean Bird*, as previously believed, and it had been transporting a cargo of mostly sugar. The ship left from Havana, Cuba, on Christmas Day 1798 and had likely been traveling back to Philadelphia before it was stranded.

Despite her extensive research on the subject, there were still many questions left unanswered, Charles said. Among them, "Why did he leave Havana on Christmas Day? What happened to the Carhart family? What is the Camphene Club? Were they [the Club] really connected with Carhart? Is there a ship OCEAN BIRD?"

Another question that remains unanswered, at least as far as public knowledge is concerned, is there even a body underneath that tombstone?

Captain Carthart's grave certainly serves as a reminder of Ocean City's long and rich maritime history, even if questions and mysteries still hang in the air surrounding one of the town's most well-known, though not initially well-documented, shipwrecks.

27

Frontier Town

In late 1950s American life, the nightly television lineup had become a revolving door of stalwart cowboys riding through unblemished landscapes of mountains and valleys as far as the eye could see. The '50s and '60s marked the peak point of nostalgia for the Wild, Wild West— *Gunsmoke* debuted in 1955, *Bonanza* in '59 and *Outlaws* in '60, among many other competing shows that glorified the debauchery and the freedom of the Old West. It was almost unavoidable, then, that the Western wave would eventually ride its way into a mid-Atlantic beach town. Frontier Town Wild West Shows opened just outside of Ocean City, in Berlin, Maryland, in 1959.

The park was built by Bill Patton and Bill Pacey and modeled after an 1860s Western town, complete with stagecoaches and a "dance hall" featuring cafeteria-style dining, along with staged gunfights and cancan shows, a Spanish-style "Calaboose" for the convicts and a steam train that carried visitors around the park's grounds. It was known in its early days for its Wild West shows, which featured dramatic reenactments of life in the Old West. To this day, parkgoers who aren't careful may find themselves caught in the middle of a gunfight in the O.K. Corral or held captive in a good, old-fashioned bank robbery.

The Wild West Show originally included real-life horsemen who would travel to Berlin in horse trailers, where they would sleep at night. The Frontier Town Campground came to be in 1963 because the horsemen needed a place to park their trailers, and housing was also needed for rodeo

Left: A postcard depicts Frontier Town's Golden Nugget Saloon. *Authors' collections.*

Below: A family poses on a stagecoach at Frontier Town. *Courtesy of David of gorillasdontblog.blogspot.com.*

riders, actors and Native Americans who sold traditional crafts and taught archery in the park.

A Cherokee actor and dancer from the park's early days, John "Red Bird" Moore, worked at Frontier Town every summer and brought his family, including children Aimee "Screaming Eagle" and John "Laughing Wolf," along with him. When the children grew up, they continued performing in the park every summer, even after their father passed away and they had found full-time work on the West Coast. The Moore family legacy of performing ceremonial dances, traditional crafts and archery lessons continues in Frontier Town to this day.

Locked up at the Frontier Town Calaboose. *Courtesy of David of gorillasdontblog.blogspot.com.*

Frontier Town's iconic stagecoach boat advertised the park to beachgoers in the 1970s and '80s, along with the Conestoga wagon boat of the 2000s. *Courtesy of Karl Schwarz.*

In 1977, Frontier Town opened its water park, and its main event, a three-flumed waterslide, was named after Red Bird, "Red Bird's Mountain." The park's first modern bathhouse also opened that year. In the 1980s, the park expanded and added a new registration office, a camp store, a pool, a laundromat and two more bathhouses.

The park has only continued to expand, and the modern, thirty-eight-acre Frontier Town includes the campground; a mini golf course; the water park, which today features a lazy river, new slides and a watering hole for the little ones; and, of course, the 1860s replica town and its Wild West shows. The town includes a stable, a rodeo corral, a church, a barbershop, a general store, two saloons, a leather shop, a general store, a mine, a train, a stagecoach, a petting zoo, a bank and a hotel.

Dancers continue to wow diners in the corral, though the park's most famous act would probably be the train robbers—actors, often teenagers, dressed as outlaws who "hold up" the train in search of gold, which they usually find under the seats of the train's youngest riders.

28

Gone but Not Forgotten

SHORE DRIVE-IN

Truckers who drove along U.S. Route 50 in late evening about three miles outside of Ocean City back in the '50s, '60s and '70s might recall a faint glow in the night sky toppling over the tree lines, accompanied by the cinematic sounds of the latest Hollywood hits. These would be a common occurrence back in the day, thanks to the Shore Drive-In in West Ocean City.

First opened in 1954 during the boom of the drive-in in the United States, the fourteen-acre property was one of the most beloved nightly attractions in the area and could hold an astounding five hundred cars at maximum capacity on busy summer nights. The theater was originally operated by William A. Carrier of West Virginia and his business partner John S. Rokisky but was taken over in 1958 by Walter Gettinger, who operated several other movie houses in the Baltimore area.

Coined the "Family Theatre," the Shore was one of roughly four thousand drive-ins in the country and the closest one to Ocean City. Back then, few establishments were operating in Ocean City where people could catch the latest Hollywood films, except for venues like the famous Capitol Theatre on Worcester Street, also owned by Walter Gettinger, which was destroyed by fire in 1964. The Shore featured famous films, such as *Fury of the Pagan*, *Doctor Faustus* and *Days of Wine and Roses*. The entrance fee for adults in the early days was well under a buck, and children under the age of twelve were always free.

Above: The Shore Drive-In sign was left to nature after the park closed. *Courtesy of kilduffs.com.*

Right: Shore Drive-In poster. *Courtesy of Earl Shores.*

The Shore Drive-In had a typical setup for the period—a large gravel lot in a horseshoe shape, with audio ports roughly every ten feet and an enormous screen that was visible from the highway. The earliest showings were usually at 7:30 p.m. and went through midnight during the summer. Guests could gorge on buttery popcorn, soda and candy at the concession stand.

Most noticeable from Route 50 was the flashy marquee sign that greeted guests as they entered the gate. Red, green and white stripes; bright neon; and backlit movie titles caught the attention of those seeking entertainment, and for many, the sign is indelible in their Shore Drive-In memories. Today, barely visible remnants of the once-lavish sign are hidden beneath weeds and brush on the side of Route 50 heading east into town.

The operation remained strong until the mid-1970s, when more traditional movie theaters started popping up along the shore, making it much more convenient for people to catch the latest blockbuster flick indoors and closer to where they were visiting. The Shore closed its front gate permanently in 1976, and the property was used afterward to host local flea markets for a while. But before long, the acreage became a distant memory. The entrance was quickly and quietly overgrown by weeds and foliage.

The Shore Drive-In sign as it stood in the late 2010s. *Courtesy of Karl Schwarz.*

The Shore Drive-In concession stand as it stood in the late 2010s. *Courtesy of Karl Schwarz.*

As of 2019, the property that was the former location of the Shore Drive-In sits abandoned and is steadily being reclaimed by nature. The original concession stand, ticket booth, restrooms and numerous other outbuildings presumably used for storage are crumbling in the thick woods, and the screen once viewed by thousands now towers over the forest in a decrepit state. Some original movie speaker junction boxes and poles are still standing with the scattered relics, but the parking lot has mostly reverted to woodland. In 2018, the property was for sale for $1.2 million, but its future remains a mystery.

HOUSE OF CRABS

Seafood restaurants are common in seaside resorts like Ocean City, and the town has certainly been home to some big players through the years. Although dozens of crab shacks and raw bars are scattered up and down Coastal Highway at any given time today, few remember those lost to history—House of Crabs being a prime example.

House of Crabs, a family restaurant located on Route 50 in West Ocean City, which was particularly well known for its crab selection, was a pillar in the Ocean City seafood lineup from the time it opened in 1973 until it closed twenty-five years later. Located just one mile past the Harry W. Kelley Drawbridge and just east of Gran Prix Amusements, the establishment was a hidden gem and the perfect place to go for "super jumbos" flown in from New Orleans, salty oysters, quality service and everything in between.

Edgar J. Altvater Jr. and his wife, Mary, proudly operated the establishment while also co-owning the National Pike Crab House in Howard County, Maryland, which opened in 1963. It wasn't until Edgar retired in 1988 that his two sons would take over the House of Crabs operation and continue its success until it closed a few years after. Interestingly, Edgar was involved in the development of an exclusive seafood spice with the help of a close friend in Baltimore who worked for the Baltimore Spice Company. Back then, it was referred to as spice no. 5102.

The inconspicuous House of Crabs building was an average-size wooden structure and was mostly rectangular, with an area that protruded at the entrance. A wood shingle roof and mid-height weathered clapboards adjoined to the façade gave the exterior a truly maritime appearance.

The inside is remembered as being dark and rustic, with nautical décor hanging on every inch of wall space. Large tables had holes in the middle

Left: House of Crabs advertises fat crabs flown in from New Orleans. *Authors' collections.*

Right: House of Crabs ashtray, circa 1980s. *Brandon Seidl.*

with waste bins below, so those enjoying crabs only needed to push their trash forward into the opening. The popular bar near the dining room regularly sat up to eleven people, while both the beer garden and dining room could seat one hundred visitors each. At full capacity, House of Crabs was a hopping place to be.

While cold pints were always important at the bar, the year-round crabs were what made the business. The family served upward of thirty-five bushels per day in season and averaged forty bushels per day during holiday weekends. Crabs were flown into what is now the Baltimore/Washington International Airport, and a truck was sent north to get them to supplement local summer and off-season crabs.

During the gas shortage of the '70s, the truck was sent with a surplus of gas on board, just to be sure it could make the round trip in time for the dinner rush. The family prided themselves on keeping essentially the same waitresses and cook staff during the entire time in business, and the operation is remembered for superb customer service.

General operating hours aligned with the rest of the town—it shut down operations during December and January to save costs. While the customers were mostly tourists during the "one hundred days of summer," locals are what kept it profitable during the off months. In fact, former Ocean City mayor Harry W. Kelley was known to be a regular and, at one point, granted the family a key to the city, citing that they had the best crabs in town. Another notable regular was John Dale Showell, a wealthy Ocean City businessman and hotel owner. He would order six of the largest crabs available and a pitcher of cold beer.

The construction of Waterman's Seafood Company in 1982 gave House of Crabs a new competitor, but it wouldn't curtail its efforts or success for years to come. Today, the Route 50 Wawa convenience store sits on the property, which was purchased from the Altvater family in 1999, but the sand below surely continues to vibrate with the sounds and energies of laughter and fun had by thousands of fulfilled guests of the House of Crabs.

SHANTYTOWN VILLAGE AND MARINA

Shantytown Village, built in 1976, was a forty-four-acre picturesque storybook village featuring fine specialty stores and restaurants on the serene waters of West Ocean City. Modeled on a quaint fishing village, the architecture was inspired by such tourist locations as Nantucket, Massachusetts, and Sausalito, California.

The small island featured upward of thirty shops in its prime, including boutiques and places to purchase anything from holiday gifts and souvenirs to collectibles, jewelry, home accessories, candy, flowers and wine. And the village didn't end with unique waterfront shopping. Delicious eateries featuring fresh-caught seafood and desserts were intermixed for those who wanted to take a break and relax while looking out over the bay with a delectable appetizer or refreshing cocktail.

Flagship eateries back then were Dockside Deli, Bluewater Grill and Something's Fishy Restaurant. Notable shops through the years, most of which were between two hundred and six hundred square feet, were Donald's Duck Shoppe, Santa's Summer Place, Mason Collection, the Lettering Works, Shamrock Shanty and the Kite Loft.

The Shantytown Village was developed by Daniel Trimper IV, the namesake and descendant of the eldest son of Daniel Trimper, founder of Trimper Rides. Daniel was well known in Ocean City for his development and real estate work. He is credited with erecting and selling some of Maryland's first condominiums. The village was built on property owned by Daniel's father, Daniel Trimper III, and was located beside the southwest corner of the Harry W. Kelley Memorial Route 50 drawbridge.

Unique to the village was a replica seventeenth-century Shantytown lighthouse, where families could enjoy beautiful views of the inlet from the observation deck. Also iconic was the oversized American flag that was visible across the bridge and beyond.

Equally famous as the shopping and eateries were the village's marina and fishing pier. Boaters would cruise across the bay and tie their boats to the docks for a day of shopping. Bait and tackle supplies were plentiful, thanks to several nearby shops, and passengers could pay for a variety of boating excursions, including fishing trips and nature cruises. Catches of the day made popular photo opportunities on any one of the headboats, the most popular being *Miss Ocean City*, while inland cruises in the waters off of Assateague Island typically occurred aboard the *Bay Queen*. Visitors were also welcome to throw a line in along the Shantytown Fishing Pier and try their luck at catching trout, tuna or flounder.

Shantytown was demolished in 2003 to make way for the development of upscale homes and condominiums.

29

Stinky Beach

S tinky Beach was once a locals' secret, hidden by Shantytown until 2003 and formally known as Homer Gudelsky Park. Today it's a popular sunbathing and fishing spot. It is tiny but still usually less crowded than the main beach across the bay.

Stinky Beach is pet friendly and a perfect place to cast a line, take a stroll or watch the boats sail in and out of the inlet. Ocean City lore says that the area used to serve as a dumping ground for the town, and the western winds would bring bugs and the smell of garbage to the beach. The water is shallow, and the wind spreads the smell of the canal, hence the name.

The little strip of beach provides a clear view of the downtown skyline, where the curving tracks of Trimper's Looping Star roller coaster is most prominent in the sky. Truth be told, there's not much of a smell, and the view of downtown Ocean City from Stinky Beach is unmatched. On a clear summer night, it can be the ideal spot to end a day exploring Ocean City and all of its incredible oddities, and because the sun rises in the east, it's also one of the best locations to catch the sun breaking over the horizon.

A wintertime view of Stinky Beach. *Kristin Helf.*

About the Authors

BRANDON **S**EIDL is a longtime enthusiast, chronicler and author of Ocean City's amusement and boardwalk history. Seidl is the creator of Trimper's Haunted House Online (www.ochh.net), coauthor of *Trimper's Rides* and cocreator of the Bill Tracy Project (www.billtracyproject.com).

KRISTIN **H**ELF is a lifelong lover of Ocean City and has been spending her summers on the Eastern Shore since babyhood. She lived on the shore for two years after college, which is when she started chronicling her adventures and discoveries in Ocean City personally and professionally. She continues to write about, photograph and share all of the magic and mystery of her favorite place. Today she's a teacher and lives in Annapolis with her husband, B.L., and their dog, Gypsy.